MARCIA ADAMS

CHRISTMAS
in the
HEARTLAND

MARCIA ADAMS

CHRISTMAS
in the
HEARTLAND

RECIPES, DECORATIONS, AND TRADITIONS
FOR JOYOUS CELEBRATIONS

Photographs by Jon Jensen
FOOD AND PROP STYLING BY FRED DERBY

CLARKSON POTTER / PUBLISHERS
NEW YORK

ALSO BY MARCIA ADAMS
Cooking from Quilt Country
Heartland
Marcia Adams' Heirloom Recipes
New Recipes from Quilt Country

Published by Clarkson N. Potter, Inc., 201 East 50th Street, New York,
New York 10022. Member of the Crown Publishing Group.

Random House, Inc. New York, Toronto, London, Sydney, Auckland
http://www.randomhouse.com/

Originally published in hardcover by Clarkson N. Potter, Inc., in 1992.

CLARKSON POTTER, POTTER, and colophon are trademarks
of Clarkson N. Potter, Inc.

Printed in Hong Kong

Design by Helene Silverman

Library of Congress Cataloging-in-Publication Data
Adams, Marcia
Marcia Adams' Christmas in the Heartland/Marcia Adams; photographs by Jon
Jensen. Includes index.
1. Christmas cookery. 2. Christmas decorations. 3. Christmas I. Title.
TX739.2.C45A33 1992
641.5'66—dc20   91-44300
ISBN 0-609-80261-5

1 3 5 7 9 10 8 6 4 2

First Paperback Edition

For all the wonderful people at WBGU-TV 27,
Bowling Green State University, Ohio—
they have become my second family.

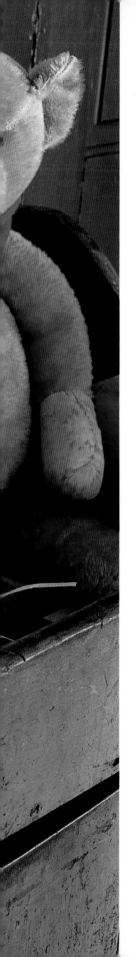

~ C O N T E N T S ~

INTRODUCTION
x

A RUSTIC COUNTRY CHRISTMAS
The Hippensteel Family
1

MORAVIAN TRADITIONS IN BETHLEHEM, PA
The Martin and Virgilio Families
33

A VICTORIAN-INSPIRED CHRISTMAS
The Mattes Family
81

CHRISTMAS AT HOME WITH FRIENDS
Marcia and Dick Adams
119

DIRECTORY
160

CREDITS
162

INDEX
163

···· ACKNOWLEDGMENTS ····

"Think where man's glory most begins and ends
and say my glory was I had such friends."
Yeats

One thing I enjoy most about my life is that I am able to share what I do with lots of people. It gives me incredible satisfaction to discover new places, people, bits of information that I find fascinating, wonderful recipes, both new and old, and to be able to pass it all on.

Two years ago, as I was busily preparing for my own Christmas, it occurred to me that some of the meaningful traditions, unusual recipes, and clever decorating ideas that I was seeing as I traveled about ought to be recorded and passed on. Each part of the country has its own regional ways of celebrating this holiday; I found them marvelous and, as always, wanted to tell everyone about them. The idea of recording what I'd seen and learned became irresistible. Pam Krauss, my editor at Clarkson Potter, gave me an enthusiastic go-ahead for the book, and Ron Gargasz, program manager at WBGU-TV 27, said, "I've been wanting to do a Christmas special—let's go for it." And so we did.

From the very beginning, I knew it was an undertaking that would require the talents of many people, all working together. I looked forward to the experience with pleasure, for as a writer I ordinarily work by myself and, as I am a gregarious soul, this project gave me an opportunity to bring together two important aspects of my life—my work and the people who are my friends and family. What I didn't realize was that I would make so many more friends

along the way. That was a lovely, unexpected bonus.

To the host families who permitted us to live with them throughout the season of Christmas, I say "thank you, thank you!" The Hippensteels, the Martins, the Virgilios, and the Matteses were unfailingly gracious and helpful. All of us so appreciated their good humor and cooperation, even as we invaded every room of their homes from eight in the morning until eleven at night.

Fred Derby, my food and prop stylist, and Jon Jensen, my photographer, were inspirational—no cookbook writer has ever been better served than I was by those gifted, hardworking people. Other individuals pitched in—Lois Hamilton, the food coordinator of my television series; Sue Clutter, who assists me here at the house with recipe testing; and Joan Fackler, another friend, who has exquisite taste and an eye for detail and who agreed to gather special props and accessories for photography. Kristy Schmitt and Gail Bryan kept the shopping done, phones answered, and computers humming. And, of course, my husband, Dick, without whom I could not function, again took care of many practical details that would have gone undone had he not been there overlooking things with his usual astute objectivity.

As we moved from community to community, we found at each site more people to help. I had never met any of them before, but because they wanted to share the traditions of their families and friends, they happily volunteered to assist. Their names are listed in the credits and we so appreciate their efforts—I will be grateful to them forever.

Denise Kisabeth, director of the PBS television series "Amish Cooking from Quilt Country" and "Heartland Cookery," plus Mark Henning and Tim Westhoven were the immediate TV crew; I had worked with them before and knew I could count on their skills as always. And all together, we produced a book and a TV show in a rather short time. On the way, something very special happened. This team of people began to interact with one another, though they all came from different artistic disciplines. A synergetic energy suffused us all, and the project began to sing.

In New York, at Clarkson Potter, the staff there took the raw material and fashioned this splendid thing you hold in your hands. Pam Krauss—I am blessed to have such a discerning and knowledgeable editor who cares so much about our shared books. Howard Klein and Jane Treuhaft thoughtfully mulled over Helene Silverman's lovely book design with me, and Mark McCauslin, the production editor, and Teresa Nicholas, the production supervisor, kept us all on schedule. Carole Berglie, the copy editor—how I admire her depth of knowledge on so many subjects. I am so grateful to Katie Workman, who took my worried phone calls, and Tina Zabriskie, who managed the intricate details of publicity. Laurie Stark oversaw it all with Carol Southern. Chris Tomasino, my agent, and Carl DeSantis, my attorney, steered me through the business end of it with great professionalism. To you all, my thanks.

Later, back at Bowling Green, Ohio, another whole crew (I call them my second family) came into the picture as we shot the studio material. Patrick Fitzgerald, WBGU-TV's manager, who watched over us all with care and, ultimately, made everything come out right; Jan Bell and Debbie Bewely, who created the very appropriate and beautiful setting for all our endeavors; Tim Smith and Pat Koehler, who arranged for special publicity and projects that so enhance the show; Tammy Griffy, my efficient and ever-cheerful floor director; the camera crew who caught every expected (and unexpected) cue: Villamore Cruz, Brian Dsyak, Steve Robinson, Vello Vannak, and Angela Shoup; the cooking crew who could whip out five soufflés or six loaves of bread in an hour—I marvel and thank them over and over again—Diana Bruns, Pat Hamad, Doris Kisabeth, and Betty Weaver.

In quiet back rooms where multiple television screens, wires, sound boards, reels, buttons, and switches reign supreme—it is all a mystery to me yet—the engineers made the show actually happen: Fred Dickinson, Nick Gorant, Cheryl Joyce, Scott Kisabeth, Bob Kreinkemp, Doug McClaflin, and Rajil Sayani. And at the desks and computers, the business part that kept the show running smoothly was attended to in a very personal way by Pat Booth, David Drury, Chris Sexton, Ardis Shirkey, and Lisa Wayne.

And I especially wish to acknowledge Tiffany & Co. of New York, who provided the handsome dishes and accessories on the set, and the generosity and support from the show's sponsors, Maple Leaf Farms, Merillat Industries, Inc., and Sauder Woodworking Company.

A project of this magnitude takes so many hands and heads and sharing of responsibilities—make no mistake about that. Maybe that was why it was all so much fun and so satisfying for us to work together, for sharing is partly what Christmas is about in this twentieth-century world, just as it played a part in that first Christmas—a sharing of what people had and without pretension. Two thousand years ago it was just a manger and some wisps of hay; but today we have other trappings—cranberries, Christmas cookies, and candles. It is the undercurrent of warmth and love in the sharing that binds us together at this magical time of year.

····· I N T R O D U C T I O N ·····

As I started to prepare for the very first Christmas my husband, Dick, and I spent together with our two sons (this was a second marriage for each of us, and we each had a child), he watched the making of the Advent wreath, the Jackson Pollock–like painting of shelf paper to use as gift wrap, the frenzy of baking, and he commented, with some wonderment and a tad of apprehension, "I never saw anybody make such a production out of Christmas."

I plead guilty. I can still remember the sheer delight I felt when I first saw that gorgeous scene in *The Nutcracker* when the magic begins and the tree grows thirty feet tall on the stage. I've been trying to duplicate that feeling in my holiday celebrations ever since. I think there *is* a magic surrounding Christmas, and the emotional dimension of the total experience is, or can be, quite tangible.

When it arrives I recognize this feeling of gladness instantly. It might come over me suddenly while shopping in a decorated store where carols are playing, or while gazing at our lighted Christmas tree sagging with ornaments collected from travels and other happy days. It has sometimes come in an early morning when, alone in the kitchen, I glance out the windows and notice in the light of the striped pink dawn that the lake is beginning to freeze over and the geese are keening overhead, flying south on their annual journey. At these moments there is a rush of warmth in my heart, and I think, "Ah, there it is, my old friend, my Christmas feeling."

It is during these December days, with or without snow, that a wondrous benevolence seems to descend upon us and we are all surrounded by an outpouring of good feeling that is part of this special time of year. Charles Dickens summed it all up: "There seems to be magic in the very name—Christmas!"

This is my favorite season; it is rich in multicultural food and decorating traditions as well as folklore. Christmas is a subject that occupies my mind, not to mention my hands, for several months every year. I shop year-round, stashing away gifts that I pick up here and there across the country, and noting them on a master list that I keep in a rather tattered Christmas file. In October I begin to bake in earnest, happily writing down plans on yellow tablets, alerting friends about dates for parties, and so on. In November, the wrapping of gifts starts and I assemble materials for decorating the house. And, of course, December crowns the whole year with its procession of good times, good food, and renewals of old friendships. Sometimes we have traveled during the holidays, and those have been exceptionally nice Christmases, too, as we observed how other cultures celebrate in their special ways.

The idea of doing a Christmas book had been lurking in my mind for some time, and from the beginning, I thought it was important to show how families celebrate according to their interests and traditions, and how these traditions were rooted in American history. I began tracing the celebration of Christmas from pagan times through Old World customs to those of the New World in America; it was an absolutely fascinating story. Our twentieth-century Christmas holiday has links to all of the above, but mostly, I discovered, to Victorian England.

I've collected these carved wooden Santas from folk artists all over the Midwest. The stocking is made from remnants of a patchwork quilt made by my grandmother.

And we have further intermixed our traditions, integrating ethnic, religious, and family customs into a holiday that is uniquely our own. I like that—it is very American, I think, to sort through it all and pick out the best.

In the homes of the families I visited, I was pleased to find yet another group of "attic receipts" that were used only during the holidays and could be updated for today's kitchens. And Christmas decorating ideas, many of them indigenous to various parts of the country, played an important role in making the celebrations you'll see here very special. I was

particularly struck by two motifs that seemed to recur over and over: the apple has played a prominent role in American Christmas celebrations throughout the decades, and the pattern of the hand has been used since the dawn of time as a decorative symbol. Each family in this book used both the apple and the hand in their foods and decorations, which I found a charming coincidence. It is just one more example of how the soul of the season can appear in different guises, yet always symbolizing the warmth, caring, and respect that binds us together during this special time.

A Rustic Country

Christmas

As a gardener and cook who uses fresh herbs, I have long known of Oris Hippensteel and the Summer House at North Manchester, Indiana—they are "just down the road," to use Hoosier parlance. I first visited Oris to write an article on her herb garden, and it didn't take long to fall under the spell of her warm, ebullient personality and enthusiasm for her favorite subject, herbs. These plants, their history, and finding ways to utilize the colorful yield of her gardens are a source of continual inspiration to her and her friends. Never is this more obvious than at Christmas.

The Summer House is supercharged with energy as the entire family makes wreaths, swags, and table and holiday decorations embellished with greens and herbs raised and gathered from right outside the door. For me and many fellow Hoosiers, a December trip to Oris's to see the clever new things she has created and the fine examples of folk art she offers for sale is an annual tradition. Her boundless imagination and her unerring eye in seeking out the best of American craftspeople make her compact workroom-cum-shop a marvel of Christmas charm and ingenuity.

The Summer House perches on the crest of a hill, surrounded by a rail fence and an extensive garden of flowers and more than 200 varieties of herbs. Even in December, the magnitude is apparent. It is an engagingly spontaneous garden that is obviously the creation of a master gardener. A full-time schoolteacher (with no fewer than three degrees), Oris is foremost an herbalist and historian.

"The Summer House is a pre–Civil War building that was used for canning, preserving, and butchering," explains Oris. "I became aware of it when I began raising herbs in the neighboring field and thought what a wonderful place it would be to have an herb shop and teach herb classes."

Not long after that, one of her children, riding by the old building on his bicycle, saw the owner drenching the structure with kerosene, getting ready to burn it down. Her son pedaled home as fast as he could, and Oris, children in tow, flew over to make an offer on the soon-to-be torched summer house. She sealed the contract with a handshake and a quarter that she borrowed from her son. The farmer's parting words: "Just make sure you keep the front lawn mowed."

The whole Hippensteel family fell to work. "To move it, we literally had to tie the place together," says spouse Bob Hippensteel. "But it has been worth the work. Lots of people look at old buildings, think they aren't useful, and tear them down. We've lost so many old fencerows and barns—it's part of our rural heritage and it's too bad so much of it is disappearing."

Each year Oris shows a collection of limited-edition Santas. This hand-fashioned figure has a white fleece robe and a face made of beeswax.

SANTA CLAUS

Santa Claus's likeness was first seen in America in 1800. At that time, he was depicted as a skinny fellow, but by 1872 his image had been fleshed out (too many sugarplums, perhaps?) to become the portly fellow we know and love today.

Though the legend of St. Nick reaches back to Asia Minor and the second century A.D., our contemporary incarnation is an amalgam of Santa traditions brought to this country by generations of immigrants.

When the Dutch came to colonial America, they brought their celebration of Saint Nicholas, just as the Germans clung to their memories of Kris Kringle. Eventually the religious and secular images merged into a symbol of generosity known as Santa Claus. Illustrator Thomas Nast, a German immigrant, created the plump and mischievous image of Santa for *Harper's Weekly* in the mid-1880s, and most of us have envisioned Santa that way ever since.

Clement C. Moore, a descendant of a prominent New York family, penned the celebrated poem "A Visit from St. Nicholas," which was printed anonymously in several newspapers and appeared in a collection of his poems in 1837. Moore's depiction of Santa as a merry elf immediately struck the fancy of his readers; coupled with Nast's artwork, the American Santa had fully evolved.

The Summer House came complete with occupants—raccoons and a nesting mother robin. "She had a condo in the corner," laughs Oris. "I didn't have the heart to disturb her, so we waited to remodel until she and her brood flew away."

Today the Summer House has been lovingly and knowledgeably restored and serves as a sales outlet for Oris's wreaths and other herb-related items, as well as a place for herb seminars. In addition, Oris is always looking for new artisans whose work is not sold elsewhere.

"The house has come full circle," says Oris. "Originally it was used for summer food preparation so the main house wouldn't be so hot from all the cooking. The family dried herbs upstairs, and now we do too." And like them, the Hippensteels use the place mostly in the summer.

ABOVE: *In the early December twilight, the Summer House is a peaceful place.* RIGHT: *The front porch, supported by stones as it would have been during the pre–Civil War period, is dotted with antique pieces— a corn dryer, an 1850 wheelbarrow filled with apples and boughs, a sled with wooden runners, and a carpenter's toolbox.*

CLOCKWISE FROM ABOVE LEFT: *Oris found this charmingly primitive handmade canvas ornament in Ohio. Pink globe amaranth attached to Styrofoam balls with a glue gun and decorated with narrow rose ribbon creates a pleasing, natural tree ornament. Two of Oris's ornament designs feature stuffed homespun hearts. Small bags of blue and white ticking are filled with Oris's potpourri mixture, tied with raffia and wildflowers, and then hung on the tree; the bags also can be used as sachets.* OPPOSITE: *This hearth in the fireplace room, dating back to 1854, sports a cooking crane and a Dutch oven, which Kerry occasionally uses for hearthside cookery. On the mantel are more of Oris and Kerry's folk art finds.*

RIGHT: *Wreaths made of fresh green herbs that later dry out can be used in the kitchen for seasoning recipes throughout the winter. Small bouquets of herb flowers provide accents of color.* OPPOSITE: *A miniature feather tree hung with antique ornaments nestles under the stairs leading to the loft. Presents are wrapped in plain brown paper tied with scraps of homespun.*

FEATHER TREES

Some call them "Charlie Brown Christmas trees," with their sparse, sometimes molting branches made of goose down. Feather trees take their shape from Germany's white pine trees, whose branches radiate out from the trunk like spokes on a wheel. The limbs grow far apart, leaving ample space to hang ornaments and burn candles safely.

The Germans are credited with devising these first artificial trees, which recall the white pine in a primitive yet stylized way, during the late nineteenth century. Goose feather tufts were cut from quills, dyed green, and dried. The bits of colored fluff were then individually wrapped with copper wire and fitted together to create small side branches. These, in turn, were arranged along a much sturdier wire to create the large boughs that would hold candleholders.

Feather trees came in all sizes, ranging from miniatures just a few inches tall to those eight feet in height. Larger models came in sections so they could be dismantled for easy storage.

How did the trees come to America? Christmas historians agree that the German wholesalers who exported exquisite and now rare blown-glass ornaments called *kugels* to the United States between 1880 and 1920 also sent feather trees. Feather trees were popular everywhere in this country by 1900, and President Theodore Roosevelt, with his interest in nature and the conservation of real trees, was an early champion of their use.

Establishing the age of a feather tree is difficult, for they were produced through the early 1950s and are now being very well replicated by contemporary folk artists. The older ones are quite rare, even those made as late as the 1950s, for after Christmas many ended up on trash heaps—they were never expensive. Until now.

At holiday time, the place bustles with activity as Oris prepares for her Christmas Open House; every spare minute is spent creating ornaments and arrangements from the flowers and herbs she raised during the growing season. The rest of the family pitches in —especially son Kerry, who also teaches school, shares his mother's enthusiasm for herbs and antiques, and is a budding gourmet cook. He makes herb jellies and vinegars and does much of the food preparation at home as well.

"I am also the gatherer of the wild rose hips; they make great wreaths," he explains, pointing to antique baskets filled with the branches of deep red berries. "I am always competing with the deer for them—it is one of their favorite foods."

In December the outside of the Summer House is swagged with fir, blue spruce, pine, holly, a bit of boxwood, and clusters of rose hips. The fireplace room has a roaring fire, and an antique stitchery above the mantel proclaims "God Bless Our Home." The original cooking cranes in the hearth still get frequent use. A Hoosier cabinet serves as a buffet when the Hippensteels entertain here; this year it is being used for the family's

Christmas brunch. A large feather tree stands in one corner, decorated with handmade ornaments collected from across the Midwest plus Oris's own creations. Gifts are wrapped in plain brown paper and homespun ribbon, as they would have been in a country house before the Civil War.

In the front parlor, smaller feather trees are hung with antique ornaments and a collection of wooden Santas designed by Oris and executed by a local artist. The large tree here is more formal, featuring crocheted baskets, dried flower balls hung from ribbons, and a Victorian hand made of fabric and decorated with ribbons and herbs— one of Oris's designs. This was the first time I had seen the hand used as a decorative Christmas motif, and I fell in love with it immediately. To my delight, I found that it was used over and over again every place we visited.

TOP: *Oris and Kerry travel all over the Midwest, seeking out regional artisans to represent in their shop.*
RIGHT: *The front parlor, built in 1890, is a gracious friendly room, with a loft for drying herbs. The fireplace screen depicting the Summer House as it looked originally was painted by a local artist.*

VICTORIAN HAND TREE ORNAMENTS

Oris adapted this ornament from one she saw hanging on a friend's Christmas tree. It requires a sewing machine. For decorating the hand, I especially like using dried baby's breath and tiny pink rosebuds. The greenery is lacapodium moss.

Whenever Oris uses a glue gun, she always keeps a bowl of ice water handy for unexpected hot drops of glue landing on tender fingers. If this happens, immerse the fingers immediately in the ice water.

MATERIALS
tracing paper
2 7 x 5-inch squares ecru cotton fabric
1 7 x 5-inch square fusible fleece interlining
ecru thread
ecru embroidery floss (optional)
8-inch length narrow ecru satin ribbon
30 inches 2-inch-wide ecru lace
assorted dry foliage and small dried flowers

TOOLS/EQUIPMENT
washable marker pen or quilting chalk
straight pins
sewing machine
iron
needle and thread
hot glue gun

1. Trace the hand pattern onto tracing paper, then transfer the pattern onto the wrong side of one ecru square. Fuse the fleece onto the wrong side of the second ecru square.
2. Pin the two squares together, right sides together, and machine-stitch along the pattern lines, including the thumb, leaving the cuff end open.
3. Trim the seams, clip the curves, turn right side out, and press firmly with a hot iron. If desired, embroider 3 lines for the finger separations through all 3 layers.
4. Turn the cuff edge under and tuck the ends of a ribbon loop inside (this will be the hanger). Machine-stitch closed.

5. Cut the lace into three 10-inch lengths and, with a needle and thread, run a basting stitch along the edge of one length. Gather and hand-stitch to the top edge of the cuff. Place the remaining 2 lengths side by side, selvage edges overlapping by ¼ inch, and baste down the center of the overlapped edges. Gather the lace to form a rosette and sew to the glove cuff.
6. With the hot glue gun, fasten the dried foliage and flowers to the center of the rosette.

MAKES 1 ORNAMENT

FRESH HERBAL WREATH

Oris makes clever miniature wreaths for napkin rings and tree ornaments, and larger versions to hang on walls and doors. The principle is the same for both. As a base, she frequently chooses young slender willow branches, which are very supple and easy to bend. Lacking willow, the conventional grape vines work well, too. In her December garden, all of the thyme plants were still colorful, as were the sages, so those were what she selected. As the wreath dries, the herbs will shrink slightly, so make the bunches generous.

MATERIALS

willow or grape vines

22-gauge florist wire

**bunches of assorted fresh herbs, such as
yellow thyme, mother of thyme, caraway
thyme, purple and green sage**

dried berries and/or flowers (optional)

TOOLS/EQUIPMENT

wire cutters

1. Twist the vines into a circle of the desired size, using thinner, more pliable vines for small wreaths, and thicker, more mature vines for larger, sturdier wreaths. Secure the first loop with wire, then form several more vine circles on top of the first, wrapping at one or more places with wire as you go.

2. Beginning at the 10:00 position and moving counterclockwise around the wreath, place the first bunch of herbs, a generous handful, stem ends down along the curve of the wreath base; attach the stems firmly with wire. Add another bunch at the 9:00 position, covering the stems and wire of the preceding bunch, and continue all the way around the wreath in this fashion.

3. When the wreath is finished, secure the stems under the first bunch and allow an extra 10 inches of wire to protrude out the front. Loop this back and forth around the wreath and pull tight. Snip off excess wire.

4. If desired, rose hips or dried flowers can be added with hot glue, though the wreath itself has a great deal of color.

MAKES 1 WREATH

HERBS AT CHRISTMAS

Herbal lore is intertwined with many Christmas legends. Rosemary in particular is mentioned frequently in Christmas tales. According to one story, a rosemary bush opened its branches to shelter Mary and Jesus from Herod's soldiers when they fled Egypt. Another story contends that Mary hung some of Jesus's baby clothes to dry on a rosemary bush; when the clothing was removed, the bush's white flowers had turned blue. For centuries, rosemary has played a significant part in Christmas celebrations; churches even used it to protect congregations from bad spirits.

Today rosemary has become a symbol of love and loyalty, and we use it in wreaths, in manger scenes, to garnish roasts and wassail bowls, as well as to season traditional holiday dishes. I like to attach a small branch of fresh rosemary to the ribbons on top of fragrant pomander balls.

Other herbs have come to be associated with the Christmas season. Lavender, said to be Mary's favorite herb, represents purity and virtue. Pennyroyal, a small-leaved evergreen mint, is sometimes called a manger herb, as is thyme, which is said to bloom at midnight on Christmas Eve. (This doesn't seem to happen in the Midwest, but I still like the story.)

Somewhat more exotic is bedstraw (*Galium verum*), a plant native to Palestine that was cut for hay and fed to livestock. Its blossom is white and scentless, but legend tells us that because the baby Jesus lay on bedstraw on Christmas Eve, the blossoms turned to fragrant gold. Bedstraw is occasionally found in some specialty herb shops during the holiday season, or you can raise your own.

Miniature grape vine wreaths decorated with fresh thyme and dried flowers are clever napkin rings; larger versions encircling candles make handsome centerpieces.

MULTIFLORAL VINEGAR

Kerry makes these attractive and flavorful vinegars for the shop, using bottles collected from antiques shops or auctions. There is no need to heat the vinegar; the warmth from sunshine does the work. The flowers will lose their color after a few days and should be discarded. Be sure to use unsprayed, organically grown flowers.

MATERIALS/INGREDIENTS

4 cups rice wine vinegar

4 8-ounce bottles with corks or lids

½ cup nasturtium flowers and buds, *or*

1 bunch (approximately 10 stems) lavender flowers, left on the stalk, *or* **½ cup pineapple sage blossoms,** *or* **½ cup rose petals, preferably the old-fashioned scented variety**

tweezers

self-adhesive labels

1. Pour 1 cup of vinegar into each of 4 attractive bottles and add several stems of a single variety of flower to each. Cover tightly and place in a sunny window for 1 week.
2. Remove the faded flowers using tweezers, recork or reseal, and label.

MAKES 4 HALF-PINTS

SPICED HONEY

Kerry makes both spiced honey and multifloral vinegar as gifts for friends, and if there is time, he makes enough to sell in the shop.

This is lovely on scones, biscuits, or toast.

MATERIALS/INGREDIENTS
5 whole cloves
5 whole allspice berries
pint jar with lid
1 pint honey
¼ teaspoon grated nutmeg
2 cinnamon sticks
plastic wrap

1. Place the cloves and allspice in a pint jar. Pour the honey over the spices and stir in the nutmeg. Add the cinnamon sticks and loosely cover the top with plastic wrap. Place the jar in a container of warm—not hot—water and allow to stand until the water is cool.

2. Remove the honey jar from the water and seal. Allow the honey to stand 1 week before using.

MAKES 2 CUPS

17

The Hippensteels are hectically involved with the shop right up to Christmas Eve —the last herb arrangement is picked up just before 8 P.M.—so Christmas morning is the family's first chance to relax in many weeks. To celebrate, they planned a Christmas brunch at the Summer House. The quiet of Christmas day in this venerable house is bliss. The golden light of morning streams through the wavy old glass-paned windows, casting yellow lozenges of light on the worn wooden floors. The fragrance of pork and caraway and potpourri scents the rooms. The house is all theirs again. When Oris says, "This house speaks to me," we know what she means.

The brunch menu, decided upon by Kerry, uses indigenous ingredients, including pork raised on their farm and eggs, apples, and corn, and emphasizes early American recipes in keeping with the Summer House's history. All of the dishes can be made in advance, an important consideration for this busy tribe. The family, ordinarily on the run from morning until night, relaxes in front of the fireplace and enjoys food seasoned with herbs from their extensive gardens. Yet before long, the conversation turns to plans for spring—after all, these are gardeners, and gardeners always live in the future.

Outside the herbs are mostly dormant, but inside, the ideas are blooming.

Bob, Seth, Kerry, and Oris Hippensteel gather in the kitchen, where yet another feather tree is hung with handmade ornaments. The stenciled border at the ceiling was designed and painted by the family.

APPLES

Apples were among the earliest Christmas ornaments. Their association with Adam and Eve made apples especially appropriate for a Christian holiday, as the Church attempted to endow pagan holidays with religious sentiment. At Christmastime, apples were still fresh and plentiful from the recent autumn harvest and they combined well with greens.

The movement of these customs across the centuries and across oceans is surely part of the romance and miracle of this holiday. When I heap a silver bowl with apples and tuck in bits of holly and spruce, I am merely reenacting those cherished customs from peasant huts all over Europe; there is so little that is really new in our world.

Today we find even more uses for the apple at Christmas, and it appears in some of our favorite winter dishes—mincemeat, steamed puddings, cakes, cookies, and hot mulled cider.

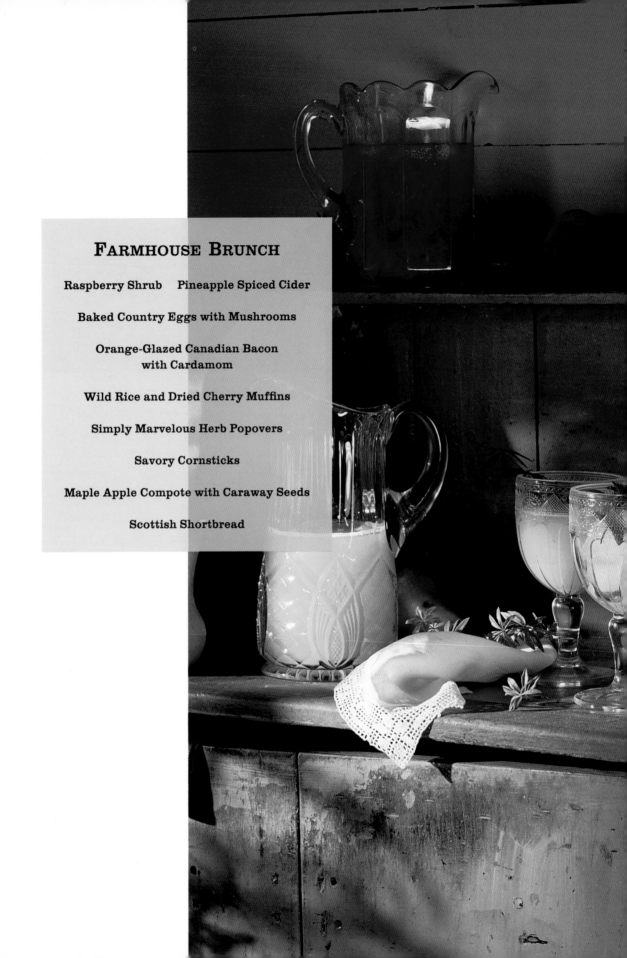

FARMHOUSE BRUNCH

Raspberry Shrub   Pineapple Spiced Cider

Baked Country Eggs with Mushrooms

Orange-Glazed Canadian Bacon
with Cardamom

Wild Rice and Dried Cherry Muffins

Simply Marvelous Herb Popovers

Savory Cornsticks

Maple Apple Compote with Caraway Seeds

Scottish Shortbread

RASPBERRY SHRUB

A shrub, derived from the Arabic word sharab, *meaning drink, is a beverage made from a fruit syrup to which water, wine, or liquor has been added. In the eighteenth and nineteenth centuries, they were used for medicinal purposes as well as refreshment. Although the original recipe called for lemon juice, in antebellum times, vinegar was used in place of costly lemon juice, and it is still a very good addition. This is a surprisingly sophisticated drink—do try it.*

1 10-ounce package frozen raspberries, thawed, or 2 cups fresh
1 cup sugar
¼ cup white wine vinegar
1 cup dry white wine or white rum, chilled
ice cubes
1 quart chilled club soda
fresh mint sprigs, for garnish

Puree the berries in a food processor or blender; strain into a small saucepan. Add the sugar and cook over medium heat until the sugar is completely dissolved, about 2 minutes. Stir in the vinegar and chill in the refrigerator until cool. Add the wine or rum. To serve, pour about ½ cup of the shrub mixture over ice in a tall glass. Fill to the top with club soda and garnish with fresh mint.

MAKES ABOUT 6 SERVINGS

A selection of breakfast beverages and a folk art Santa in a cozy fur-trimmed parka share the stage on a quaint old dry sink enhanced by the original paint.

PINEAPPLE SPICED CIDER

Tired of the usual Bloody Marys? This nonalcoholic mixture, anise-flavored, is an adaptation of a very old drink from a period when pineapple was an extravagance. It is a wonderful brunch beverage.

SPICED SYRUP

6 whole cloves

1 heaping teaspoon anise seeds

1 cup water

⅓ cup sugar

JUICE MIXTURE

1 46-ounce can unsweetened pineapple juice, chilled

½ cup orange juice, chilled

1 750-milliliter bottle sparkling apple juice, chilled

ice cubes

fresh woodruff or mint, for garnish

Tie the cloves and anise seeds in a 6-inch square of cheesecloth. In a small saucepan, combine the water, sugar, and spice bag and bring to a boil; lower the heat, cover, and simmer for 5 minutes; cool. Remove the spice bag, squeezing any liquid back into the pan, and discard. Transfer the syrup to a jar and refrigerate.

To serve, combine the juices and spiced syrup in a 2-quart pitcher. Pour into ice-filled glasses and garnish with woodruff or mint.

MAKES 10 6-OUNCE SERVINGS

BAKED COUNTRY EGGS WITH MUSHROOMS

This dish is one of my favorites because it is tasty and creamy and yet so easy to prepare in advance. It could also be served as a light luncheon offering. I like to serve it with a bit of meat on the side—pork, generally, such as sausage patties cut into decorative shapes or Canadian bacon.

5 tablespoons unsalted butter

2 cups halved fresh mushrooms

1 tablespoon finely chopped onion

2 tablespoons finely chopped green pepper

3 tablespoons all-purpose flour

1½ cups milk, heated

1 tablespoon finely minced fresh parsley

1 teaspoon low-sodium chicken stock powder

½ teaspoon curry powder (or more, to taste)

¼ teaspoon salt

¼ teaspoon freshly ground white pepper

6 large hard-cooked eggs, peeled

½ cup buttered dark bread crumbs

2 tablespoons finely minced fresh parsley, for garnish

Preheat the oven to 350° F. Over medium heat, melt 2 tablespoons of the butter in a medium saucepan. Add the mushrooms, onion, and green pepper, and sauté until the mushrooms begin to brown, about 5 minutes.

In another medium saucepan, melt the remaining 3 tablespoons butter. Add the flour and cook over medium heat, stirring, until the mixture bubbles up. Add the milk all at once, whisking smooth, and cook until the mixture bubbles up in the center. Add the parsley, chicken stock powder, curry powder, salt, and pepper, and cook over low heat for 2 minutes. Remove from the heat and set aside.

Butter a shallow gratin dish (7 x 10 x 3 inches) or a flat 10-inch round casserole. Quarter the eggs and arrange in the dish, yolk side up. Stir the mushroom mixture into the white sauce and pour over the eggs. Sprinkle the crumbs over the top and bake for 40 minutes, or until the top is golden brown and bubbly. Sprinkle with the parsley to serve.

Note: This recipe can be doubled, using a 3-quart flat dish.

MAKES 6 SERVINGS

SIMPLY MARVELOUS HERB POPOVERS

Popovers, with their chewy crusts and puffy centers, are first cousins to cream puffs and make a great addition to the hot roll basket at any brunch. Serve them piping hot with lots of butter. This version is delicately seasoned with parsley and thyme.

1¼ cups milk, at room temperature
1¼ cups all-purpose flour
¾ teaspoon salt
⅛ teaspoon cayenne pepper
3 jumbo eggs, at room temperature
2 tablespoons minced fresh parsley
⅓ teaspoon dried thyme

Preheat the oven to 425° F. In a medium mixing bowl, combine the milk, flour, salt, and cayenne and beat with a rotary beater or wire whisk just until thoroughly blended; don't overbeat. Add the eggs one at a time, beating after each addition until completely blended. Stir in the parsley and thyme.

Grease 6 popover cups and fill three-quarters full with the batter. Bake for 20 minutes, then reduce the oven temperature to 325° F. and continue baking 15 to 20 minutes longer, or until the popovers are golden brown. Serve immediately, for they fall quickly.

MAKES 6 LARGE POPOVERS

WILD RICE AND DRIED CHERRY MUFFINS

The addition of nutty wild rice and dried tart red cherries to a muffin batter sweetened with honey yields a delightful holiday breakfast bread. The mace is almost unidentifiable but makes the flavor quite special. Never overmix muffins—it creates tunnels in the finished product.

If you use paper muffin liners, it is best for this recipe to first coat the liners with vegetable oil spray.

½ cup (1 stick) unsalted butter, softened
½ cup honey
1 large egg
2 cups all-purpose flour
3 teaspoons baking powder
¾ teaspoon salt
¼ teaspoon mace
1 cup cooked wild rice, unseasoned
1 cup milk, at room temperature
1 teaspoon vanilla extract
1 cup dried tart cherries

Preheat the oven to 400° F. In a mixer bowl, cream together the butter, honey, and egg; it will not cream as a butter-sugar mixture does, but it should be blended well. By hand, lightly mix in the flour, baking powder, salt, mace, and rice. Combine the milk and vanilla and fold into the batter, then gently fold in the cherries.

Fill greased or paper-lined muffin cups two-thirds full of batter. Bake for 20 to 25 minutes, or until the muffins are golden brown. Serve hot with butter.

MAKES 18 MUFFINS

ORANGE-GLAZED CANADIAN BACON WITH CARDAMOM

A delicate orange sauce flavored with cardamom is a fresh new accompaniment for Canadian bacon. The meat cooks gently in the sauce and every slice is well seasoned; a brown sugar glaze is added just before serving. This is perfect with any egg dish.

1¼ pounds Canadian bacon, sliced ¼ inch thick (about 20–22 slices)
¼ cup light brown sugar, packed
½ teaspoon dry mustard
½ teaspoon ground cardamom
¼ teaspoon freshly ground black pepper
1½ cups orange juice
3 bay leaves
2–3 tablespoons light brown sugar, for glaze

Preheat the oven to 325° F. In a greased shallow 2-quart (12 x 7-inch) baking dish, arrange the bacon slices in 2 overlapping rows. Combine the brown sugar, mustard, cardamom, pepper, and orange juice in a small saucepan; bring to a boil and boil 1 minute. Pour over the meat and arrange the bay leaves on top. Bake uncovered for 25 minutes.

Remove the bacon from the oven and pour off and discard all but ¼ cup of the pan juices. Preheat the broiler.

Sprinkle 2 to 3 tablespoons brown sugar over the bacon and place the bacon in the broiler, about 5 inches from the heat, for approximately 5 minutes, or until the bacon is glazed and bubbly. Serve immediately.

MAKES 6 TO 8 SERVINGS

SAVORY CORNSTICKS

These elegant, light cornsticks with a subtle touch of sage always elicit such enthusiasm that it is worth giving the cupboard space to the special cast-iron pans. Serve with spiced honey.

1¼ cups stone-ground yellow cornmeal
½ cup sifted all-purpose flour
2 teaspoons sugar
2 teaspoons baking powder
¾ teaspoon salt
½ teaspoon ground sage
¼ teaspoon coarsely cracked black pepper
1¼ cups buttermilk at room temperature
¼ teaspoon baking soda
1 large egg, beaten
⅓ cup vegetable oil

Preheat the oven to 475° F. Grease 2 cornstick pans and place them in the oven to heat. In a large bowl combine the cornmeal, flour, sugar, baking powder, salt, sage, and pepper. Combine the buttermilk and baking soda in a small bowl and stir into the dry ingredients. Add the beaten egg and beat vigorously for 1 minute. Add the vegetable oil and blend. Spoon the mixture into the heated pans and bake for 12 to 15 minutes, or until golden. Invert the sticks onto a warm platter.

MAKES 12 CORNSTICKS

SCOTTISH SHORTBREAD

This is a buttery, delicate, melt-in-your-mouth cookie. Because they're not too sweet, I especially like them with a fruit compote or ice cream. In some parts of the country, this shortbread was also called kumfit. This recipe can be made in either pie tins, cake pans, or cookie molds. For extra flavor, dip the pointed ends of the cookies into melted chocolate morsels and allow to cool on wax paper.

¾ cup (1½ sticks) unsalted butter, softened
⅓ cup confectioners' sugar
⅓ cup cornstarch
2 tablespoons finely minced candied ginger
½ teaspoon salt
½ teaspoon powdered ginger
1½ cups all-purpose flour

Preheat the oven to 325° F. In a large mixer bowl, beat the butter slightly, then add the confectioners' sugar and cornstarch gradually, beating until the mixture is pale and fluffy, about 3 minutes. Blend in the candied ginger, salt, and powdered ginger; gradually add the flour. Don't overwork the mixture—the dry ingredients should just be incorporated.

Transfer the dough to a greased 10-inch pie tin and pat out to about ¾ inch thick. Make a bit of crimped edge, like pie crust, and smooth the top. With a spatula, ease the edges away from the sides of the pan, leaving ¼ inch of space. If the dough is too soft to work, put it in the refrigerator for 15 minutes.

With a sharp knife, score the dough halfway through into 16 pie-shaped wedges. With a fork, prick the center of each wedge twice. Chill for 30 minutes if the dough is very soft.

Bake for 30 minutes, or until the shortbread just begins to color—some color is important for flavor. Remove from the oven, allow to cool for 10 minutes, then cut through the scored lines. Allow the pieces to remain in the pan until completely cool.

MAKES 16 SHORTBREADS

MAPLE APPLE COMPOTE WITH CARAWAY SEEDS

This is a precious old recipe that dates back to colonial times, when maple syrup, honey, and caraway seeds as well as apples were always on hand in kitchens. This dish tastes as wonderful today as it did then. When it is baked, the apples turn amber and appear almost candied.

I especially like Jonathan apples for this dish. Serve with crème fraîche or a bit of sour cream.

1 cup maple syrup
½ cup honey
1 tablespoon fresh lemon juice
½ teaspoon ground cinnamon
¼ teaspoon caraway seeds
speck of salt
4 cups peeled, cored, and quartered small, firm
  cooking apples (approximately 7)

Preheat the oven to 350° F. In a small saucepan, combine the maple syrup, honey, lemon juice, cinnamon, caraway seeds, and salt. Bring the mixture to a boil, cover, and set aside to let the flavors blend while you prepare the apples.

Arrange the apples in a greased oval gratin dish approximately 9 x 12 inches. Pour the hot sauce over the apples and bake, uncovered, for 30 minutes. Turn gently with a rubber spatula twice during the baking period, being careful not to break up the apples.

Allow the apples to stand at room temperature for 2 hours before serving; they will continue to absorb the syrup.

MAKES 6 SERVINGS

MORAVIAN TRADITIONS IN

BETHLEHEM, PA

I first visited Bethlehem during a very hot July. I was absolutely bowled over by the architecture of the old stone Germanic buildings, as well as the fine Federalist ones. The community dates back to the Revolutionary War, when the town was the site of the Continental Army's hospital; General Washington, John Adams, and Thomas Jefferson were regular visitors to the town. Bethlehem was my first introduction to the Moravians and their holiday customs. However, I was equally delighted with the ethnic ambience of the city, a reflection of the multicultural work force that found employment at Bethlehem Steel. We were told repeatedly, "You must come back at Christmastime to *really* see Bethlehem." And when I did, I knew it was a treasure, a repository of holiday traditions and customs at once unique and universal.

Founded by a small group of Moravians from Europe, this picturesque community perched on the bank of the Lehigh River in eastern Pennsylvania received its evocative name on Christmas Eve, 1741. According to a diarist in the congregation, the colonists met in a small log house, part of which "was used for cattle. Because of the day and in the memory of our dear Savior, we went into the stable in the 10th hour and sang with feeling, so our hearts melted." From that night on, the town was called Bethlehem.

The Moravians were members of the Unity of the Brethren, one of the oldest Protestant denominations in the world. They named their sect for their homeland, since they had migrated from Moravia and Bohemia, which are now provinces of Czechoslovakia.

For the first hundred years, the settlement remained exclusively Moravian. The original community was segregated according to age and sex, and the groups lived in what were called choirs, each with its own building, hymns, and liturgy. Active as missionaries in the wilderness, the Moravians established a unique relationship with the Native Americans, treating them equally as "true believers" under one God. From the beginning, they tuned their whole lives to the sound of music —from sunrise to sunset, in the fields, at the table, on journeys, at christenings, weddings, and funerals, and especially at Christmas.

In the nineteenth century, the community was opened to others, and in the early twentieth century immigrants arrived in Bethlehem from throughout Europe, many to work in the mills of Bethlehem Steel. Irish, Germans, Czechs, Italians, Slovaks, Poles, Hungarians, and others settled on the south side of the town, near the steel mills, across the Lehigh River from the Moravians, who had settled on the north side.

But at Christmas, the town is one. The entire month of December revolves around the mingled traditions of the holidays. This is the time to make the spicy and crisp Moravian cookies (sometimes called ginger thins) as well as sugar cakes, actually a tender yeast bread dappled with brown

An illuminated Moravian Advent Star, RIGHT, five-pointed with eight rays, shines on porches throughout the historic district and in hundreds of homes beyond.
ABOVE: Bethlehem citizens dressed in authentic Moravian costumes offer guided tours of the district for interested visitors.

sugar and butter, and Moravian mints, delicate sugar mints in assorted colors. Treasured recipes are brought out from old card files and cookbooks, and the cooking and baking begin.

Another Moravian custom is for families to call on one another to view each other's homemade Nativity scenes, or *putzes,* a word derived from the German *putzen* (to decorate), used only among American Moravians. The early Moravians celebrated Christmas by building *putzes* in their houses. On Christmas morning, children gathered around the crèche as their parents narrated the story of Christ's birth. The tradition of the *putz* still flourishes in Bethlehem, and the *putzes* range from intricate to simple. Many are works of art, filled with antique, hand-carved animals and figures from Moravia, placed in a pastoral setting of fresh evergreens, moss, and driftwood.

In the ethnic neighborhoods on the south side of the river, traditional European dishes of the holiday such as Welsh saffron bread, pasties, biscotti, and homemade pasta are lovingly prepared.

Bethlehem in December glows with candle-light and the sweet smell of beeswax—every house in the historic district has a hand-dipped candle at each window. Overlooking the city and the Lehigh Valley is the enormous Bethlehem Advent Star, 81 feet high and 53 feet wide. From the beginning, the symbol of this American Bethlehem was the Advent Star, a many-pointed version that originated at a Moravian boys' school in Germany in about 1850.

With the diverse beginnings of the Moravians and the other immigrants—and the resulting mix and the meetings of the two separate communities—Bethlehem has become a very special place to live and to visit.

BELOW: *Many Bethlehem families still create a* putz, *a Nativity scene in miniature, in their homes each season. This elaborate presentation at the home of Alice and Francis Knouss fills a small room and includes rocks, wood, moss, evergreens, lights, and hand-carved figures.*

LOVEFEASTS

The lovefeast is primarily a Moravian Church song service, opened with prayer, that reminds the Brethren congregation of the family bond that unites them. The service concludes with a simple meal that is not consecrated.

Sacristans pass trays of slightly sugared yeast buns (made from the same dough as the traditional Moravian Sugar Cake) to the worshipers in their pews. When all have been served, men of the church distribute mugs of coffee, tea, chocolate, or orangeade, all served quietly and without interruption of the singing.

The minister eats his bun and coffee, and the congregation follows. Music is continuous except for prayers. The service is held several times a year and, of course, at Christmas. It is an uplifting, sociable event that draws not only Moravian and non-Moravian residents of Bethlehem, but many seasonal visitors to the town as well.

Above, sacristans Mr. and Mrs. Mark Parseghian ready coffee and baskets of love buns for one of the Central Moravian Church's holiday lovefeasts.

POLLY HECKEWELDER DOLLS

Polly Heckewelder was an actual person—the daughter of the Reverend John Heckewelder, a famous Moravian missionary who worked among the Indians. Born in 1781, only the second white child to be born in the state of Ohio, she later lived in Bethlehem.

The dolls that bear her name are made by the Ladies' Sewing Society of the Central Moravian Church. The society was formed in 1861 to do relief work during the Civil War and was originally called the Soldier's Relief Society; after the war, the name was changed to the Ladies' Sewing Society, and so it remains today.

The first doll was made in 1872, and all thereafter have been numbered. Dressed in a pink or blue frock just as Moravian girls were in early days, each doll is intricately detailed. The dolls' little hats, called *schnebbelhaube*, are exact replicas of the hats still worn by many Moravian women when they attend church; the color of ribbon used on the caps (which matched their bodice laces) indicates which choir they belong to—married women use blue ribbon, single women, pink; young women wear red ribbons, and widows, white. The dolls' faces are painted on and, when soiled, can be replaced—a Moravian facelift?

Each Polly Heckewelder doll requires approximately eighty hours of work, and there is a two- to three-year waiting list.

The women of the Ladies' Sewing Society meet year-round to work on the treasured Polly Heckewelder dolls, each of which bears an individual number. There are never enough of these coveted dolls to fill all the orders.

ABOVE: *Lemon leaves attached to a Styrofoam base with pearl stick pins make a sophisticated, stylized wreath for hall sconces.* BELOW: *A portrait of an early Moravian matron soberly oversees the guest book in the entry hall.*

The Martin Family

Roger and Susan Martin and their daughters, Katie, age twelve, and Emily, age nine, live in a special house in Bethlehem, where Roger is president of Moravian College. Built of regional dark-toned brick and called the John F. Frueaf (*free-aff*) House, the home was built in 1819 in Federal architectural style and sits squarely on the sidewalk; the deep door and mullioned wide-silled windows are typical of the architecture of Bethlehem's Historic District.

The interior of the house has been carefully restored, with a wide center hall running from front to back; the living room, with its fireplace and an antique clock made by the well-known Christian Bixler family (circa 1710–1840), looks as it might have 150 years ago. Yet with the comings and goings of the Martins' preteen daughters and their friends, plus the Martins' active social life connected with the college, the house is very much a part of this century.

"Bethlehem is very special at Christmas," says Susan. "I had heard how beautiful the vespers were, with all the congregation holding lighted beeswax candles at the end of the service, but when I saw it the first time, I was completely overwhelmed by the music and the candlelight. It was so dramatic and moving—unforgettable."

Susan, a self-described Air Force brat, is blond, pretty, and petite, and handles her role as college president's wife with charm and aplomb. Both Martins are energetic and gracious, not to mention well organized. For them, the whole month of December centers on Moravian College's Christmas vespers, which are held three times every weekend in the Central Moravian Church. Roger and Susan entertain each time, having people in either before or after the concerts.

Because the house is so purely Federalist, Susan

*Roger and Susan Martin man the head of the table and offer tea as guests
make their way around the cookie-laden table.*

decorates with some restraint, in keeping with the period. Magnolia leaves, greens, and fresh pears are arranged on sideboards, accented with clusters of the unusual glass Christmas ornaments that are available at the Moravian Book Store. Pale mauve and green ribbons intertwined with greens line the curving hall staircase, echoing the tones in the Oriental carpet.

The girls create cones of nuts, mints, dried fruits, and cookies, using a twentieth-century glue gun to prepare an eighteenth-century design as popular today as it was then. Susan makes several tender Moravian Christmas cakes in advance and freezes them.

It is also time to bring in a supply of locally made beeswax candles, another regional Christmas craft. The whole town has a faint fragrance of honey during December.

ABOVE: *Simple greenery and grosgrain ribbons entwine a banister.* RIGHT: *At Christmastime, the Martins turn the secretary-desk into a display case for their daughters' favorite things, including their Polly Heckewelder dolls.*

MORAVIAN MINT CONES

These make stunning centerpieces, reminiscent of stylized topiaries. The mints can be ordered by mail (see Directory), or simply substitute assorted pastel-hued after-dinner mints.

MATERIALS
4 Styrofoam cones, 6–10 inches
200–300 multicolored mints
bits of greenery (optional)

TOOLS/EQUIPMENT
newspaper
hot glue gun
small bowl of ice water

1. Spread newspaper over your work surface. Place a cone in the center.
2. Apply a dab of hot glue to the back of a mint and press it onto the base of the cone. (If you accidentally burn your fingers, immediately dip them in the ice water.) Continue to affix additional mints, working upward to the top of the cone and placing them as close together as possible.
3. Finish, if desired, by randomly gluing small snippets of greenery amid the candies.

MAKES 4 CONES

Variations

Almost any natural material can be used to make these graphic cones. Suggestions to try include a mixture of nuts and dried fruits, crisp cookies (both pictured opposite), pinecones, leaves, seed pods, berries, and so on. If you are combining materials of varying sizes, as in the fruit-and-nut cones, alternate rows of the larger pieces with rows of smaller ones to avoid leaving gaps of exposed cone. Fill in any remaining spaces with greenery.

ABOVE: *The Martins enjoy introducing friends and colleagues to Moravian holiday treats.* **BELOW**: *Susan avidly collects this gold-banded blue and pink china, embellished with scenes from Moravian College, and uses it for entertaining.* **ABOVE RIGHT**: *Decorated trees stand sentinel over the dining room table.*

After the Sunday afternoon vesper service, Susan sometimes serves desserts, including Moravian specialties. The dining room is spacious, with a lighted beeswax candle in each window, and dominated by a long Queen Anne table. Antique silver platters lighted by tiny Moravian candle clips are filled with more cookies and mints and surrounded by glossy lemon leaves. The antique china is red and white, patterned with scenes from the college. The feeling is traditional yet up to date.

While the parents congregate with their adult acquaintances in the dining room, Katie and Emily entertain their friends in the living room, serving hot chocolate from a table that once belonged to George Washington and using their mother's collection of demitasse cups gathered from her years of living abroad.

The logs in the fireplace crackle, the beeswax candles scent the rooms, and dusk falls along with gentle powdery snow. Across the river, the Advent Star glows in the twilight, sending its beams out across the valley.

Katie Martin and her younger sister, Emily, prepare hot chocolate for their friends in front of the fireplace in the living room, while their parents entertain the adults in the dining room. The cocoa, said to be one of Thomas Jefferson's favorite evening drinks, is made by adding a chocolatey base to hot milk.

Christmas Cookie Tea
After Moravian Vespers

Moravian Ginger Thins   APEAS Cookies

Moravian Sand Tarts

Moravian Sugar Cake

Half-Moon Cakes

Moravian Mints (See Directory)

Thomas Jefferson's Hot Chocolate

Hot Tea and Coffee

MORAVIAN GINGER THINS

The ideal Moravian ginger cookie is as thin and crisp as a potato chip, delicately flavored with molasses and spicy with ginger, cinnamon, and cloves. They have been baked in this country since 1766, when members of the Unity of Brethren Church settled in North Carolina and named their community Salem, after the Hebrew word for peace, shalom. *I was told truly fine ginger cookies should be so thin that it takes a dozen of them to make a mouthful—now that's thin!*

In pioneer times, these cookies were baked in huge quantities and stored in sixty-pound lard pails. All the bakers I spoke to in Bethlehem said it takes two people to make the cookies—one to roll out the dough and cut the cookies, the other to watch them in the oven and remove them to cooling racks. After making them, I agree: they are so thin, they burn easily and require full-time monitoring. Besides, it's more fun that way! To keep the dough cold, many Bethlehem bakers roll it out on slabs of chilled slate.

⅓ **cup solid vegetable shortening**

1 cup dark molasses

½ **cup firmly packed dark brown sugar**

**1½ teaspoons baking soda dissolved in
2 tablespoons hot water**

½ **teaspoon ground cinnamon**

½ **teaspoon ground cloves**

½ **teaspoon ground ginger**

½ **teaspoon mace**

1 teaspoon orange extract

1 teaspoon salt

4 cups all-purpose flour

Melt the shortening and transfer to a large mixer bowl. Add the molasses, brown sugar, and dissolved baking soda; blend. Add the spices, orange extract, and salt; blend again. Gradually add the flour and mix well, using your hands if necessary to work in all the flour. Wrap the dough in plastic, refrigerate, and allow to "ripen" overnight or for several days.

Preheat the oven to 350° F. Divide the dough into fifths and, refrigerating the remainder, place one fifth of the dough on a floured surface. Lay a large piece of plastic wrap on top of the dough, and roll out as thin as possible.

Cut the dough into shapes with assorted floured cutters. Transfer to parchment-covered cookie sheets and bake until very light brown, about 4 to 5 minutes, watching them very carefully. You may have to reverse the sheets to ensure that the cookies brown evenly. Allow the cookies to remain on the sheet for 2 minutes, then remove them to a rack to cool.

Continue rolling and baking the remaining dough as above. Store in tins.

MAKES 8 DOZEN COOKIES

LEFT: *Dried figs, dates, and nuts are princely fare when served on Susan Martin's Georgian silver salver.*

MORAVIAN SAND TARTS

These delicate little sugar cookies, always made at Christmastime in Bethlehem, are each traditionally topped with a dusting of sugar and cinnamon and a pecan half. But the cookies are really too good to save just for the holidays; serve them year-round as an accompaniment to sorbets or ice cream.

1 cup (2 sticks) unsalted butter, softened
1 teaspoon vanilla extract
½ teaspoon salt
1¼ cups confectioners' sugar
3 medium eggs, or 2 jumbo
½ teaspoon baking soda
2 cups all-purpose flour
¼ cup granulated sugar
1 teaspoon ground cinnamon
1 egg white, slightly beaten
approximately 75 pecan halves

In a large mixer bowl, cream the butter, vanilla, salt, and confectioners' sugar until fluffy, about 3 minutes. Add the eggs, one at a time, beating well after each addition. Add the baking soda and then the flour in 2 parts, mixing well after each addition. Chill the dough overnight, or for several days.

Remove the dough from the refrigerator to soften about 30 minutes before rolling out. Preheat the oven to 350° F. In a small bowl combine the granulated sugar and cinnamon. On a floured surface, roll out half the dough about ⅛ inch thick, and cut out cookies with a 2-inch cutter.

Transfer to a parchment-lined or lightly greased baking sheet. Brush the cookies with some of the beaten egg white, then sprinkle on some of the sugar-cinnamon mixture. Press a pecan half into the center of each cookie. Bake in the upper third of the oven for 7 to 10 minutes. (The cookies will bake faster on dark pans.) Remove to a rack to cool.

MAKES ABOUT 6 DOZEN COOKIES

CHRISTMAS COOKIE HINTS

This time of year, when cookie baking is a national pastime, questions arise, especially as old heirloom recipes are pulled out of files and used with new fats and different flours. If you are using an older recipe, I have found unbleached flour most closely resembles the flours used by our grandmothers and will yield a moister cookie. Substituting vegetable oil in part for lard will also make a softer cookie.

You can use almost any type of fat in drop and bar cookies, with the exception of soft-style or diet margarines; they contain too much water and the dough will not be workable. I get better results from cookie doughs that have been made with vegetable shortenings, including margarine, by chilling the doughs overnight, then rolling or dropping them. If I have used corn oil margarine or oil, I freeze the dough for at least three hours before using.

Store crisp and soft cookies separately; if you store them together, they all get soft. I find soft cookies should be layered with wax paper or they will cling together. Cookies that have been frosted with cream cheese frostings should be stored in the refrigerator but brought to room temperature before serving.

Susan decorates a footed glass dish of Moravian Sand Tarts with a lit beeswax candle.

HALF-MOON CAKES, OR WINTER CAKES

The recipe for this traditional Moravian holiday treat is more than 150 years old, and no one knows where the custom of frosting one half with chocolate and one half with orange originated. The cake itself resembles a soft yellow sponge cake and has a very nice texture. Half-moon cake pans are in the shape of a long cylinder cut in half, about 3 to 4 inches in diameter and about 12 inches long. They are rather hard to find (see the Directory for a mail order source), so I make this cake in a 15 x 12-inch jelly roll pan, cut the cake into 2½- to 3-inch rounds, then cut the rounds in half.

½ cup (1 stick) unsalted butter, at room temperature

1 cup sugar

¾ teaspoon salt

1 teaspoon vanilla extract

3 large or jumbo eggs, at room temperature

1½ teaspoons baking powder

1½ cups all-purpose flour

⅔ cup milk, at room temperature

Quick Chocolate Frosting (recipe follows)

Quick Orange Frosting (recipe follows)

Preheat the oven to 350° F. In a large mixer bowl, cream the butter, sugar, salt, and vanilla for 3 minutes. Add the eggs, one at a time, beating well after each addition. Quickly blend in the baking powder, then add the flour and milk alternately, beginning and ending with the flour.

Pour into a buttered pan and bake for 20 to 25 minutes, or until the top is golden. Cool for 10 minutes in the pan, then tip out on a rack to cool. Slice about ½ inch thick (if using the traditional pan) or cut into rounds (approximately 20) and halve. Frost the slices with half chocolate frosting and half orange frosting.

MAKES 20 TO 40 CAKES

Quick Chocolate Frosting

6 tablespoons (¾ stick) unsalted butter, softened

2 egg yolks

2 tablespoons milk

1 teaspoon vanilla extract

¼ teaspoon salt

3 tablespoons cocoa powder

3 cups confectioners' sugar

In a mixer bowl, beat the butter, egg yolks, milk, vanilla, and salt together until smooth. Add the cocoa powder and confectioners' sugar and continue beating until well combined and smooth.

MAKES SCANT 4 CUPS FROSTING

Quick Orange Frosting

½ cup (1 stick) unsalted butter, softened

2 teaspoons grated orange zest

¼ teaspoon orange extract

¼ teaspoon salt

3½ cups confectioners' sugar

¼ cup orange juice

1 tablespoon milk

In a mixer bowl, beat the butter, orange zest, extract, and salt together until blended. Alternately add the confectioners' sugar and the orange juice and milk, and continue beating until well combined and smooth.

MAKES SCANT 4 CUPS FROSTING

MORAVIAN SUGAR CAKE

This coffeecake is one of the Moravians' classic recipes and an outstanding yeast bread. The ingredients always include potatoes, and the indentations on the top of the cake are always filled with brown sugar, cinnamon, and butter. It can be made in advance, frozen, then reheated before serving.

The dough is rich and tender and makes a most attractive bread. (This same dough is used as a base for two other Moravian specialties: Love Buns and Butter Semmels.) Many bakers make this in square pans, and it is available that way year-round in Bethlehem. However, baking the cake in a round shape gives each person more of the cinnamon-butter topping and less crust.

1 small potato, peeled and cubed

1 cup water

1 package active dry yeast

⅓ cup granulated sugar

⅓ cup unsalted butter, melted

1½ teaspoons salt

½ teaspoon grated nutmeg

3–3½ cups all-purpose flour

3 tablespoons cold unsalted butter, in ½-inch cubes

½ cup dark brown sugar, packed

1 teaspoon ground cinnamon

In a small saucepan, cook the potato in the water until very soft, about 20 minutes. Cool to lukewarm. Transfer ¼ cup of the potato cooking water to a small bowl, add the yeast, and mix with a fork; set aside.

Mash the potato thoroughly in the remaining cooking liquid until there are no lumps, adding more water if needed to make 1 cup. It should have the texture of cooked oatmeal. In a mixer bowl, combine the potato, yeast mixture, sugar, butter, salt, and nutmeg, and mix well. Beat in 1 cup of the flour, then cover the dough with a tea towel and let rise in a warm place for 45 minutes, or until it is spongy.

Stir down the dough and add enough of the remaining flour to make a soft dough. Turn out onto a floured surface, or use a dough hook, and knead for 4 minutes. Shape the dough into a ball, place in a buttered bowl, and turn once to butter all sides. Cover with a tea towel and let rise for 45 minutes, or until doubled.

Punch down the dough and turn out onto a floured surface. Divide the dough in half; cover both portions and let rest for 10 minutes. Cut parchment paper to fit the bottom of two 9- or 10-inch round cake pans and butter the paper. Roll the dough halves out into 9- or 10-inch circles to fit the pans, and transfer them to the pans, patting the dough into place right to the edges of the pans. Cover each cake with a tea towel and let rise 45 minutes, or until not quite doubled, but puffy.

Preheat the oven to 350° F. With your thumb (you can get more butter and sugar in a thumb hole, say the old-timers), gently make indentations in the top of the dough—don't poke through the dough to the bottom of the pan—at ½-inch intervals. Place a small piece of butter in each hole.

Combine the brown sugar and the cinnamon in a small bowl. Sprinkle over the top of the cakes and bake 20 to 25 minutes, or until the cakes are deep golden brown and the butter is bubbling in the center. Let the cakes cool in the pans for 10 minutes before transferring to serving plates. Cut in wedges and serve warm.

MAKES 2 CAKES, EACH SERVING 6 TO 8

Variation: **Love Buns**

Make the dough as above. After it has risen the second time, punch down the dough and divide into 12 pieces. Shape each piece into a ball, place on a greased cookie sheet, and flatten slightly. Cover the buns with a tea towel and let them rise again until doubled, about 45 minutes. Preheat the oven to 375° F. With a razor or sharp knife, cut an *M* in the top of each bun. Brush the tops with melted butter, sprinkle granulated sugar on top, and bake the buns approximately 20 to 25 minutes, or until lightly browned.

MAKES 12 LARGE BUNS

Variation: **Butter Semmels**

Make the dough as above. After it has risen the second time, punch down the dough, and on a lightly floured board, roll out the dough ¼ inch thick. Brush with melted butter and cut into 2-inch squares. Fold the 4 corners of each square toward the center, pressing the dough firmly into place. Transfer to a greased baking sheet about 2 inches apart and let rise until light, about 45 minutes. Bake at 450° F. for 20 minutes, or until golden. Remove from the oven, brush with additional melted butter, and sprinkle with confectioners' sugar. Serve hot with coffee.

MAKES 30 SEMMELS

APEAS COOKIES

This delicately flavored sugar cookie, half firm, half soft, can be sprinkled with colored sugars, if desired. Or omit the sugar and top with an English walnut half, making it an Eagle cookie. Traditionally, though, the initials AP are cut into the top of the cookie with the tip of a sharp knife. In colonial days, these were made with brown sugar and molasses and baked in pie tins. It yielded an enormous cookie, but no one minded!

1 cup (2 sticks) unsalted butter, softened

1½ cups granulated sugar

3 large eggs

¼ cup heavy cream or evaporated milk

1 teaspoon salt

1 teaspoon baking soda

1 teaspoon cream of tartar

2 teaspoons vanilla extract

approximately 5 cups all-purpose flour

English walnuts or colored sugars, for garnish

Position the oven rack in the upper third of the oven; preheat the oven to 375° F. In a large mixer bowl, beat the butter and sugar together for 3 minutes. Add the eggs, one at a time, beating well after each addition. Then add the cream or evaporated milk, salt, baking soda, cream of tartar, and vanilla extract; blend.

Add the flour gradually; you may have to mix in the last cup by hand—the dough will be quite stiff. Divide the dough into fourths, and roll out about ⅛ inch thick on a floured surface, one fourth at a time, refrigerating the rest. Cut out cookies with a 2-inch scalloped cutter and top with an English walnut half or colored or plain sugar, or make an *AP* on top of each cookie with the tip of a sharp knife.

Transfer to parchment-lined (or ungreased) baking sheets and bake for 5 to 6 minutes, or until the cookies are firm and pale yellow on top and just beginning to brown on the bottom; do not overbake. Cool on a rack.

MAKES ABOUT 6 DOZEN COOKIES

THE MYSTERY OF APEAS

These cookies date back to 1832, with a name that puzzles even the most adroit historians. According to a popular interpretation, Ann Page was a professional Philadelphia baker who stamped her initials on her cookies before she baked them. Another theory holds that the term is a corruption of the term "a piece of cake," because in those early years cookies were known as cakes. And some old manuscripts do call them APEAS. Those cookies were large, made with brown sugar, and baked in greased pie tins or cut with round scalloped cutters.

Food historian William Woys Weaver maintains that the original cookies were *Änis Plätzchen,* or anise cookies, and stamped *AP* to distinguish them from cookies with caraway. A great many bakers sold APEAS cookies to children on the streets—including Ann Page. So the story muddles on.

THOMAS JEFFERSON'S HOT CHOCOLATE

This is an exceptional recipe for hot chocolate, a beverage that Thomas Jefferson enjoyed drinking before bedtime, as he recorded in his journals. The chocolate base, similar to a soft, rich frosting, can be kept refrigerated for up to a week and then added to hot milk, a heaping tablespoon per cup. Grind a bit of fresh nutmeg over each cup before serving. This is perfect with Christmas cookies or buttered toast fingers.

Do not heat the base and the milk together in the microwave, or the mixture will become grainy.

CHOCOLATE BASE
2½ ounces unsweetened chocolate
½ cup cold water
pinch of salt
¾ cup sugar
1 cup heavy cream
1 teaspoon vanilla extract

5 quarts milk, heated
freshly grated nutmeg, for garnish

In a heavy saucepan, combine the chocolate and water over medium heat, and cook until the mixture is dissolved, smooth, and thick, whisking out any lumps. Add the salt and sugar and continue cooking and whisking for 3 to 4 minutes. Remove from the heat and allow to cool.

In a chilled bowl, whip the cream and vanilla together; stir into the cooled chocolate mixture. Transfer to a quart container and store in the refrigerator.

To make the hot chocolate, place a heaping tablespoon of the chocolate mixture in each cup (or the equivalent of what you need in a serving pot). Add 1 cup of hot milk per serving, and whisk until smooth and frothy. Grate nutmeg on top of each serving.

MAKES 20 SERVINGS

The Virgilio Family

For most residents of Bethlehem, the holiday season begins at Advent, and a flurry of entertaining starts as the *putzes* are set up, cookies are baked, and candles are installed in all the windows. But for Bob and Susan Virgilio, who live in the Historic District in a restored 1845 Federalist house they operate as a bed and breakfast, entertaining seems to be a year-round occurrence, with appreciative guests filling the bedrooms and hurrying downstairs every morning to enjoy the creative breakfasts the couple prepares.

Both Virgilios appreciate old houses and had had their eye on this particular one for a long time. When it came on the market they bought it, renovated it (it had no electricity), and opened it to the public as a bed and breakfast with spacious, sunny rooms, gracious hospitality, and exceptionally good food. "Having a bed and breakfast inadvertently made us ambassadors for the town," says Susan, "though we are constantly discovering new things about it as our guests come back and relate their experiences and how Bethlehem has touched them."

The Virgilios entertain frequently, sometimes inviting their house guests to stay for dinner, as well as playing host to their personal friends, many of whom they met at Lehigh University. Susan, who is Irish, and Bob, whose parentage is both Italian and Russian, combine all the foods of their childhood when they entertain—and never more so than at Christmas; the menus are eclectic and sophisticated.

"Even though we are Roman Catholic, we certainly wouldn't miss the Moravian vesper services," says Susan. "This year we took our son,

Rumrousal and Biscotti provide a nice excuse to sit down and relax in front of the fire.

Calvin, to the Children's Lovefeast at the church —they all were served Moravian cookies and hot cocoa in the pews. There are so many traditions here that we all share, whether we are Moravian or not."

A Virgilio family tradition is making cookies and other simple crafts with Calvin and his friends from nursery school. This season Susan created handsome gingerbread bowls to be filled with cookies or ornaments and given as gifts or used as decorations.

The stained-glass gingerbread cookies are adorable and delicious; the fun part for the tots is getting to smash up the hard candies. Susan advises doing this on a weekend afternoon and asking some other mothers to help.

Stenciling windows by dabbing a simple mixture of soap and water over doilies is another one of those easy crafts so dear to children's hearts— how many of us remember doing that in our own kitchens on paned doors and windows? The nice thing is that it is so easy to clean up afterward.

ABOVE: *The kitchen wreath is decorated with small beeswax ornaments and wheat stalks.* LEFT: *The Virgilios' kitchen takes on a festive air with greenery and a tree trimmed with cookies, apples, and locally made beeswax ornaments.*

CHRISTMAS GINGERBREAD BOWL

Fill these attractive bowls with assorted Christmas cookies; they make charming gifts. A narrow red grosgrain ribbon could be threaded from star to star in the border, tied with a bow, and decorated with a bit of greens. These sturdy bowls can be made well in advance.

MATERIALS/INGREDIENTS

1 cup (2 sticks) unsalted butter, softened
¾ cup firmly packed dark brown sugar
½ cup granulated sugar
⅓ cup light molasses
¾ cup dark corn syrup
2 teaspoons vanilla extract
3 large eggs
8½ cups all-purpose flour
1 tablespoon baking soda
1 teaspoon salt
1 teaspoon ground cinnamon
1 teaspoon ground cloves
1 teaspoon ground ginger
1 teaspoon orange extract
½ teaspoon ground allspice
½ teaspoon freshly ground black pepper

TOOLS/EQUIPMENT

mixer
2 large bowls
whisk
plastic wrap
1½-quart ovenproof glass bowl
aluminum foil
vegetable cooking spray
miniature star-shaped cookie cutter
baking sheet

1. In a large mixer bowl, cream the butter and sugars until fluffy, about 1 minute. With the mixer running, add the molasses, corn syrup, vanilla, and eggs, one at a time, beating until the mixture is well combined. In another large bowl, combine the remaining ingredients with a whisk.

BELOW LEFT: *An ovenproof bowl is smoothly covered with foil, then coated with cooking spray.*
BELOW RIGHT: *Gingerbread dough is trimmed to fit the bowl.*

2. Add the flour mixture gradually to the creamed mixture (the dough will be very stiff and you may have to use your hands to get all the flour worked in). Divide the dough into quarters and wrap each in plastic wrap. Chill overnight.

3. Cover the outside of a 1½-quart ovenproof glass bowl with a lipped edge with aluminum foil, bringing the foil over the edges to the inside. Make sure the foil is on very smoothly. Spray the entire bowl with vegetable cooking spray and set aside.

4. On a floured surface, roll one-fourth of the dough into a circle ¼ inch thick. Immediately lift the dough and press it onto the outside of the bowl, molding it firmly to the shape of the bowl without stretching it. Trim the dough around the edge of the bowl with a sharp knife, then, using a small star-shaped cutter, cut out stars around the lipped edge of the bowl about 1½ to 2 inches apart and about 1½ inches up from the bottom of the inverted bowl. Refrigerate the bowl for 1 hour; this firms up the dough and prevents slippage during baking.

5. Preheat the oven to 350° F. Place the inverted bowl on an ungreased baking sheet and bake 20 to 30 minutes, or until lightly browned and firm to the touch. Allow the gingerbread to cool on the bowl. When cool, carefully loosen the foil and lift the foil and gingerbread shell off the bowl. Peel away the foil and discard; store the shell, uncovered, in a dry place away from the humidity of the kitchen.

6. Use the remaining dough to make 3 more bowls, or cut with decorative Christmas cutters into cookies. Bake the cookies on a lightly greased baking sheet for 8 to 10 minutes, or until they are lightly browned.

MAKES 4 GINGERBREAD BOWLS, OR 1 BOWL AND 6 DOZEN SMALL COOKIES

BELOW LEFT: *Decorative shapes are cut from the bowl.* **BELOW RIGHT:** *The finished bowl, filled with cookies, is next to a wooden tree form of Advent candles.*

CHRISTMAS SNOW FOR WINDOW DECORATING

Looking for something to do with small children that is easy and can be made from materials you already have in your house? This charmingly nostalgic window decoration is in a lot of adults' memory banks. Only mild soap flakes will whip up properly, so buy accordingly. Each paper doily can be used only two times, so buy plenty, or cut your own.

MATERIALS/INGREDIENTS
½ **cup lukewarm water**
½ **cup plus about 2 slightly rounded**
    tablespoons mild soap flakes or granules
transparent tape
assorted doilies or homemade "snowflakes"

TOOLS/EQUIPMENT
mixing bowl
whisk or electric beater
small sponge

1. In a medium mixing bowl, combine the water and soap flakes or granules. Stir to dissolve, then whip by hand or with an electric beater until the mixture looks like stiff meringue and holds its shape.

2. If making your own snowflake stencils, fold several large pieces of heavy paper in fourths. Fold in half again to make a pie-shaped wedge, and use sharp scissors to cut out shapes—the more shapes and the closer together the better. Unfold and flatten out before proceeding.

3. Tape paper doilies or stencils to the inside of the window and use the sponge to dab the whipped snow over the perforations. Remove the doily or stencil immediately and allow the design to dry.

4. To remove after the holidays, simply wipe off with window cleaner and a soft cloth.

MAKES ENOUGH TO COVER
6 SMALL PANES

BEESWAX CRAFTS

Hand-dipped candles as well as Christmas tree ornaments made of beeswax are crafts unique to Bethlehem at holiday time. Robert and Lucille Smith are the town's "candle" people, making them by the thousand every year. A sideline is their ornaments, which resemble tasty maple or butterscotch wafers; a tree hung with them has an engaging hand-crafted look.

Robert is a retired pharmacist. His father, who owned the local drugstore, taught him the technique of candle dipping in 1929, when he was eight years old. The family made and sold beeswax candles for years—at one time providing all the candles for the Central Moravian Church.

Today, Robert and Lucille teach this colonial art at the 18th Century Industrial Area every Christmas. All that is needed, says Robert, is melted beeswax, which is then poured into a specially designed candle mold. It takes from seven to ten minutes for the wax to cool and harden. It appears more complex than that, but of course, the Smiths are truly experienced.

GINGERSNAP STAINED-GLASS COOKIES

These are very crispy, spicy, and colorful cookies, ideal for hanging or propping, for they are also sturdy. Prepare the cookie dough a day or two in advance and refrigerate. This is a wonderful kiddie cookie—the kind that becomes a tradition because it is so memorable. Prop them on window sills to truly appreciate the stained-glass effect.

¾ cup (1½ sticks)) unsalted butter or
   margarine

¾ cup sugar

½ cup light molasses

2 tablespoons water

3¼ cups all-purpose flour

1 teaspoon baking soda

1 teaspoon salt

1 teaspoon ground ginger

½ teaspoon ground allspice

½ teaspoon ground cinnamon

9 fruit-flavored lollipops, 3 each red, yellow,
   and green

In a large mixer bowl, cream the butter and sugar until fluffy, about 1 minute. Blend in the molasses and water. In a medium bowl, whisk together the flour, baking soda, salt, and spices; add to the butter mixture and mix well. Cover and refrigerate overnight.

Prepare the candy. Leaving the lollipops in their wrappers, place one color at a time in a small plastic bag. With a hammer, crush the candy finely. Remove the wrappers and transfer the crushed candy to small dishes, keeping each color separate.

Position the oven rack in the upper third of the oven; preheat the oven to 375° F. Roll out the dough on a floured surface (it will be quite soft) until ⅛ inch thick.

Cut out cookies using large cutters. Transfer the cookies to foil- or parchment-lined cookie sheets and, with a small cookie cutter or a sharp knife, cut out and remove designs from the center of each cookie.

With a teaspoon, fill the cutouts rather scan-tily—not clear to the top—with the crushed

candy. If you wish to use the cookies as hanging ornaments, stick half a wooden toothpick into the top of each cookie to create an opening. Remove the toothpick after baking.

Bake 5–6 minutes, or until the cookies are firm and the candy is melted. Slide the foil or parchment off the cookie sheet. When the cookies are completely cool, gently remove the cookies and store in tins, or thread each with a ribbon and hang on the tree.

MAKES ABOUT 3 DOZEN 4-INCH OR 5-INCH COOKIES

ABOVE AND OPPOSITE: *Crushed hard candies are spooned into cut-out gingerbread shapes; the finished stained-glass cookies strut their stuff along a sunny windowsill.*

Decorating the Christmas tree is a job for many hands, so Susan and Bob invite their friends over to help. It is also a good time to entertain with a holiday dinner. The children are included, so the evening is a lively one. Dinner, with Italian specialties and a nod to the Welsh, is served first, the table centerpiece being a nontraditional montage of Italian vegetables arranged on a bed of moss. "I don't like being predictably conventional," laughs Susan, her girlish ponytail bobbing as she talks. "This arrangement seemed a nice change from pine and candles."

After dinner, rumrousal and biscotti are served in the living room, while the guests bedeck the tree with glass ornaments that the Virgilios have collected through the years. Bob brings in a classic Italian dessert—zuccotto—and while the guests gather around the buffet to be served this lovely domed chocolate confection, the sound of carolers outside singing "O Little Town of Bethlehem" fills the room.

OPPOSITE: The generous buffet is arrayed on an antique lace cloth. **BELOW LEFT:** *The tree-decorating crew lines up for a festive dinner menu of Italian Stuffed Beef Tenderloin and Polenta Stars.* **BELOW RIGHT:** *The centerpiece of fresh vegetables is comprised of a Styrofoam base covered with moss, then topped with kale leaves, assorted vegetables, cut pomegranates, and strands of ivy and pine boughs. It is a nice change from conventional pine and candle arrangements.*

TREE-TRIMMING PARTY MENU

**Italian Stuffed Beef Tenderloin with
Roasted Red Pepper and Garlic Sauce**

Polenta Stars

**Tossed Fresh Winter Greens with
Cumin Vinaigrette**

Welsh Cakes   Zuccotto

Biscotti   Rumrousal

POLENTA STARS

Susan adapted this Italian favorite for a Christmas buffet dish. The sun-dried tomatoes add texture and color, and the presentation and flavor are quite perfect with the beef tenderloin. This can be made two days in advance, with the stars cut and refrigerated until serving time.

2 cups water
1 cup half-and-half, approximately
1 cup yellow cornmeal
¼ cup olive oil
1 medium onion, finely chopped
½ cup chopped oil-packed sun-dried tomatoes
1 bunch fresh basil, minced
¼ teaspoon cayenne pepper
1 teaspoon salt
2 cups grated sharp provolone cheese

In a deep, heavy saucepan, bring the water and 1 cup of half-and-half to a boil. Add the cornmeal in a slow stream, whisking constantly until a creamy consistency has developed. Cook, uncovered, for 30 minutes on the lowest possible heat, continuing to whisk until the polenta is very smooth and creamy. It should be the consistency of oatmeal. Add more half-and-half if it is too thick.

Meanwhile, heat the olive oil in a small skillet over medium heat. Add the onion and sauté until soft, about 2 to 3 minutes. Add the tomatoes, basil, pepper, and salt. Sauté until the fresh basil is wilted. Stir the onion mixture into the polenta and mix well.

Lightly oil a platter or cookie sheet and pour the mixture onto it. Shape into a rectangle about 9 x 7 inches and about ¼ inch thick. Refrigerate, uncovered, until firm.

Preheat the oven to 350° F. Cut the polenta into star shapes or rectangles and place on a greased foil-lined cookie sheet. Sprinkle the stars with the cheese and bake for 5 minutes, or until the polenta is heated through. Turn the heat up to broil to brown the cheese, which will take about 2 minutes. Watch it carefully so it doesn't burn.

OPPOSITE: *Baskets of fruit and pinecones beneath the kitchen tree.* **ABOVE**: *Polenta Stars are topped with cheese, then arranged on a platter.*

MAKES 4 TO 6 SERVINGS

ITALIAN STUFFED BEEF TENDERLOIN WITH ROASTED RED PEPPER AND GARLIC SAUCE

Certainly one of the most festive cuts of meat to serve during the holidays, beef tenderloin immediately conjures up images of lavishness and goodness. This recipe combines the best of Italian cooking, with garlic, roasted red bell peppers, porcini mushrooms, and rosemary. The fragrant sauce is quite thick and can be served on the plate beside the meat. Roast the garlic and red peppers a day in advance.

SAUCE

2 large whole heads of garlic, unpeeled

5 tablespoons olive oil

4 large red bell peppers

½ teaspoon salt

½ teaspoon freshly ground black pepper

1 teaspoon finely minced fresh rosemary

⅓ cup dry vermouth or white wine

FILLING

¼ cup olive oil

2 shallots, minced

1 green bell pepper, julienned

½ pound fresh mushrooms, finely minced, or 3 ounces dried porcini mushrooms, soaked in 2 cups warm water for 45 minutes, drained, cut into thin strips, and patted dry

2 teaspoons minced fresh rosemary

½ cup finely chopped fresh parsley

MEAT

1 3-pound beef fillet, butterflied

salt and freshly ground black pepper

6 fresh rosemary sprigs

2 tablespoons olive oil

fresh rosemary, for garnish

To roast the garlic, preheat the oven to 350° F. Cut off the tops of the garlic heads to expose the cloves. Place them in a small foil-lined pan and drizzle 1½ teaspoons of the olive oil over each. Cover with foil and bake for 1 hour, or until the garlic cloves are very tender. Uncover and allow the garlic to cool until it can be handled, about 15 minutes. With your fingers, squeeze the garlic pulp onto a small plate and divide in half.

To roast the red bell peppers, preheat the broiler with the rack approximately 6 inches from the heat. Core the peppers, cut them in half, and flatten them out in a foil-lined baking pan. Rub the surfaces liberally with 2 tablespoons of the olive oil. Broil the peppers for 10 to 12 minutes, turning occasionally, or until the skin is black and charred. With a spatula, transfer the peppers to a small brown paper sack and allow to steam for 15 minutes. With a sharp knife, peel away the charred skin and discard.

Place the red peppers and half the garlic pulp in a food processor bowl with the remaining 2 tablespoons olive oil and the salt and pepper. Process until smooth and set aside.

In a deep skillet or sauté pan, heat the oil for

the filling over medium heat, add the shallots, and sauté until they are golden, about 3 minutes. Add the green bell pepper, remaining garlic pulp, mushrooms, and rosemary and sauté until the green pepper begins to soften, about 5 minutes; it should still be a bit crisp and bright green. Let the filling cool, then stir in the parsley.

Preheat the oven to 425° F. Line a shallow baking pan with foil and coat it with vegetable spray. Place the opened fillet flat in the pan and sprinkle it with salt and pepper to taste. Place three-fourths of the filling lengthwise down one side of the fillet and flip the other side over it to cover. Tie the fillet at 1-inch intervals with kitchen string. Place the rosemary sprigs on top of the fillet, tucking them under the string. Rub the meat and rosemary with the olive oil. Insert a meat thermometer. Bake for 10 minutes, lower the heat to 350° F., and bake for 15 to 20 minutes longer for rare, or 25 to 30 minutes for medium-rare.

Meanwhile, finish up the sauce. Place the remaining filling in a small saucepan and add the red pepper–garlic puree, the teaspoon of rosemary, and the vermouth. Cook, stirring, over medium heat; it will be quite thick, so don't let it burn.

Let the fillet rest for 10 minutes, then slice it ¾ inch thick, discarding the string, and arrange on a bed of rosemary. Serve with the warmed sauce on the side.

MAKES 6 TO 8 SERVINGS

TOSSED FRESH WINTER GREENS WITH CUMIN VINAIGRETTE

Cumin, balsamic vinegar, and grated lemon zest give this vinaigrette a sprightly flavor—it is quite nice over any combination of greens. For the best texture and color, use at least three kinds.

1 shallot, finely minced
½ teaspoon grated lemon zest
1 teaspoon stone-ground mustard
¾ teaspoon ground cumin
1 tablespoon balsamic vinegar
⅓ cup fresh lemon juice
⅔ cup olive oil
8 cups assorted torn greens, such as Boston, oakleaf, or ruby lettuce, endive, spinach, etc.

In a small jar, combine all of the ingredients except the greens, and shake until the dressing is well mixed. Refrigerate several hours so the flavors can develop.

In a large bowl, toss the greens together, then drizzle the dressing over the greens. Toss lightly until well combined.

MAKES 6 SERVINGS

WELSH CAKES (*TYSEN CYMREEG*)

During the 1830s and the 1850s, poor economic conditions in the mining area of Wales motivated droves of miners to migrate to America. Many of them settled around Bethlehem, and with them came old country recipes for pasties, saffron bread, and these unforgettable Welsh cakes. They are generally served at tea time, dripping with butter, and I like to serve them at brunch, lunch, and dinner instead of rolls. They resemble miniature English muffins, and their texture is that of a rather firm cake. The currants add character and color. Lightly flavored with mace, these cakes are absolutely irresistible.

2 cups all-purpose flour
½ cup sugar
1½ teaspoons baking powder
½ teaspoon mace
½ teaspoon salt
¾ cup (1½ sticks) cold unsalted butter or
 margarine
1 cup dried currants
2 large eggs
¼ cup milk
½ teaspoon vanilla extract

In a large bowl, combine the flour, sugar, baking powder, mace, and salt. Cut the butter into 10 to 12 pieces and work it into the flour mixture with a pastry blender until fine crumbs form—the mixture should look like pie pastry. Stir in the currants.

In a small bowl, whisk the eggs, milk, and vanilla together until blended. Pour over the dough and stir until just mixed; it will be fairly sticky, like cookie dough. Preheat an electric frypan to 315°–325° F.—low to medium heat. (The Welsh use a heavy flat iron griddle called a *planc*.)

Turn the dough out onto a well-floured surface and sprinkle with some flour. Flour a rolling pin and lightly roll the dough out to ½ inch thick. With a 2½- to 2¾-inch biscuit cutter, cut out 16 cakes.

Spray the frypan with a bit of vegetable oil, and wipe it out with a paper towel, leaving just a gloss of oil in the pan; you have to do this only once. Fry the cakes about 5 to 6 minutes on each side, until they are a deep brown. Serve warm with lightly salted butter.

Note: To reheat, place cakes in a single layer in a foil packet, sprinkle with just a bit of water, and heat for 10 minutes in a 375° F. oven.

MAKES 16 CAKES

Zuccotto is garnished with pomegranate seeds and chopped pecans.

ZUCCOTTO

This dramatic yet easy-to-prepare dessert is a specialty of Florence. Its name refers to its domelike shape, reminiscent of the cupola of the Duomo, designed by Brunelleschi. Zuccotto used to be found only in Florentine pastry shops and cafés, but now you are apt to find it all over Italy. It's a nice addition to American tables as well.

This can be made up to two days in advance using a purchased pound cake as the base, then dusted with sugar and cocoa just before serving. Seductively rich, it is a boffo ending to an Italian dinner.

½ cup chopped pecans

1 teaspoon vegetable oil

salt

1 12-ounce pound cake

⅓ cup amaretto liqueur

3 tablespoons Cointreau or other orange
   liqueur

⅔ cup miniature semisweet chocolate bits

2 cups heavy cream

⅓ cup confectioners' sugar

4 teaspoons light corn syrup

2 teaspoons vanilla extract

2 tablespoons confectioners' sugar and
   2 tablespoons cocoa, for dusting, *or*
   additional chopped pecans

Preheat the oven to 375° F. Place the pecans on a shallow pan, drizzle with the oil, sprinkle lightly with salt, and toss to mix. Toast the pecans until golden brown, about 5 minutes, stirring once. Set aside to cool.

Line a 1½-quart round-bottomed bowl with plastic wrap. Cut the pound cake into seventeen ⅜-inch slices and then cut each slice in half diagonally, creating 2 triangles. Place the cake triangles close together in a jelly-roll pan. Combine the liqueurs in a measuring cup and drizzle evenly over the cake.

Place a triangle of cake against the inside of the bowl (with the point of the triangle touching the middle of the bottom of the bowl), and repeat until the inside of the bowl is completely lined with cake. Alternate pieces with and without crust to create a sunburst pattern when the cake is unmolded. If there are gaps, fill in with pieces of moistened cake. Reserve the leftover cake pieces; they will be used later (in other words, don't eat them).

Coarsely chop ⅓ cup plus 1 tablespoon of the chocolate bits in a food processor. In a chilled mixer bowl, combine the cream, confectioners' sugar, corn syrup, and vanilla, and whip until the cream is very stiff. Fold in the pecans and chopped chocolate chips. Divide the mixture into 2 equal parts.

Spoon half of the chocolate cream into the cake-lined bowl, spreading it evenly over the entire cake surface, leaving a well in the center.

Melt the remaining chocolate bits in the microwave or over warm water, cool slightly, and fold into the remaining half of the whipped cream mixture. Spoon it into the cavity, completely filling the center. Even off the top of the bowl, trimming away any protruding pieces of cake. Top the mixture with the remaining cake pieces and cover the bowl with plastic wrap. Refrigerate overnight, or up to 2 days.

To serve, remove the top layer of plastic wrap, cover the bowl with a flat serving dish, and invert the dessert onto the plate. Lift off the bowl and carefully remove the plastic wrap. Refrigerate until serving time. Combine the confectioners' sugar and cocoa in a sprinkler jar or sifter and sprinkle the top and sides of the zuccotto just before serving, or sprinkle with additional chopped pecans. Cut into wedges.

MAKES 12 SERVINGS

BISCOTTI

These versatile little toasts, literally "twice baked," are delightfully flavored with walnuts and anisette as well as aniseed. The dough is formed into small loaves, baked, sliced, and lightly toasted, then served cold. You will find biscotti a refreshing change from the usual Christmas cookies; they are just the thing with a cup of coffee when you need a little time out all to yourself. I shall be eternally grateful to Susan for this recipe.

The dough must be refrigerated at least three hours or overnight before baking.

2 cups sugar
2 cups chopped walnuts, toasted
1 cup (2 sticks) unsalted butter, melted
¼ cup aniseed
¼ cup anisette liqueur or orange juice
2 tablespoons water
2 teaspoons vanilla extract
6 large eggs
1 teaspoon salt
1 tablespoon baking powder
5½ cups all-purpose flour

In a large mixer bowl, combine the sugar, walnuts, butter, aniseed, liqueur, water, and vanilla. Add the eggs one at a time, mixing briefly after each addition. In a large bowl, whisk together the salt, baking powder, and flour; blend the dry ingredients thoroughly into the egg mixture. Cover and refrigerate at least 3 hours, or overnight.

Preheat the oven to 375° F. Divide the dough into 5 pieces. Grease 2 baking sheets. Squeeze and pat each piece of dough into a loaf ½ inch thick, 2 inches wide, and 16 inches long. Place the loaves 4 inches apart on the cookie sheets. Bake for about 20 to 25 minutes, or until the loaves are firm. Transfer to a wire rack to cool completely.

Preheat the oven to 375° F. Cut the loaves diagonally into ½-inch slices and arrange the slices on an ungreased cookie sheet, cut side down. Bake for 7 minutes on one side, then turn the biscotti with a spatula and bake for 3 to 4 minutes on the second side. The biscotti will be very crisp and golden. Cool completely and store in airtight tins.

MAKES 160 PIECES

RUMROUSAL

Rumrousal is a hot elegant milk punch, pale amber in color and perfect with Christmas cookies or fruitcake. It does pack a bit of a wallop, but a gracious one. Generally it is served hot from a punch bowl, but I find it is also very good served cold and presented in antique water glasses or short cocktail glasses. And if you serve it cold, you don't have to heat the milk—just combine everything and chill.

2 cups light rum
1½ quarts milk
¾ cup honey
½ cup bourbon

In a large heavy pot, combine all of the ingredients and stir over medium low heat until the milk is scalded—bubbles will form around the edge of the pan and a skin will form on the top. Reduce the heat and simmer for 1 minute. Strain through a fine sieve into a punch bowl and serve hot in glass punch cups.

MAKES 18 3-OUNCE SERVINGS

BOWL OF CHEER

The punch bowl, also known as the flowing bowl, has long been a symbol of hospitality. Mixing spirits, especially rum, with sweet ingredients is a typically early American tradition that arrived right after the *Mayflower* and has been around ever since. Rum was a favorite alcoholic drink in both Europe and America during the colonial period because of its low cost and its versatility in all sorts of beverage combinations.

George Washington kept his Continental Army supplied with liquor (it was safer to drink than the water) for both the warmth and, as one historian writes, "Dutch courage." Today, these old punch recipes are best served after dinner as a palate soother, or at a dessert buffet.

A VICTORIAN-INSPIRED

CHRISTMAS

For a number of years, I lived close to an 1885 Italianate house that belonged to a crusty old gentleman by the name of Mr. Gatchell. He used to sit on his front porch in a bentwood rocker and chat with the neighbors who passed by. He had a small orchard in the side yard, and every autumn I went there to gather fruit to use in my grandmother's recipe for gingered pears. Afterward, Mr. Gatchell and I would talk, sitting in the sunshine on the sagging porch, and he'd reminisce about his farming days—he was the person who taught me that baby chicks are called "peeps." He still kept a few chickens, and we could hear the roosters crowing in the morning, a most reassuring sound to a former farm girl.

For our children, his home was a favorite place to "Trick or Treat"; they called the place the haunted house, but certainly the old farmer always treated them with gruff approval and handed out Snickers bars—and pears, too, I think. When he died, the roosters no longer

American primitive antiques, they longed for a home that would properly showcase their prized possessions. When Mr. Gatchell's house came up for sale, they bought it without hesitation.

Their contractor had looked it over and said ruefully, "I can't help you. You know how this should be done, and how it should look is all in your head. But I don't know what to do." This didn't stop the intrepid and optimistic couple.

crowed at dawn and we all felt a sense of loss. Mr. Gatchell's house stood empty for a while, and then we heard it had been purchased and a new family was moving in.

It was apparent from the beginning that these new occupants were knowledgeable about authentic Victorian architecture. Each time I drove by, I marveled at the skillful improvements. When I finally met the Mattes family, the house was finished and I was absolutely dazzled by what they'd accomplished.

George and Linda Mattes had always lived in contemporary houses, but as avid collectors of

Within two weeks, they had begun the restoration themselves. The house was finished seven years later, a stunning example of what research, hard work, and love can create.

The home is full of light, warmth, comfort, and charm, reflecting the Mattes family's interests as well as their philosophy of caring and sharing both within the family circle and without; they are active in many community, school, and church affairs. And never is the Mattes house more delightful than at Christmas, as four generations congregate to prepare for the holidays.

Since the house is decidedly Victorian in flavor,

ABOVE: *Angie's bed is hung with a single-diamond hand-knitted canopy. The 1855 coverlet is handwoven.* OPPOSITE: *The stately Mattes home in its simple Christmas finery.*

and Linda is active in a group known as the Settlers that is devoted to preserving early American handicrafts, the Mattes family's Christmas is a combination of both early American and Victorian decoration and food; it is a mixture that works admirably well.

For the holidays, the Mattes house is bedecked from top to bottom with decorations accumulated over the years. In the front parlor with its tall ceilings, a large arborvitae that was overpowering their backyard now stands in for a conventional pine Christmas tree. Hung with *kugels,* blown-glass ornaments from Germany, as well as other antique ornaments and strands of glass beads, it is just one of several decorated trees in the house. This is obviously the residence of dyed-in-the-wool Christmas enthusiasts!

ABOVE: *The formal Christmas tree in the front parlor is strung with antique ornaments and glass beads, a favorite decoration during Victorian times.* RIGHT: *This Noah's ark, from Vailliancourt Folk Art in Sutton, Massachusetts, is one of the favorites among the many the Mattes family has collected.*

ABOVE LEFT: *Lollipops and hard candy toys glitter invitingly on the dry sink.* ABOVE RIGHT: *Each December the back stairway landing is transformed into a Christmas corner.* BELOW LEFT: *The upstairs landing is also a play room, filled with antique toys and, at this time of year, a collection of Santas.* BELOW RIGHT: *Rose hips decorate a wild branch wreath over the fireplace. A live tree is potted in an old butter churn and will be planted outside after the holidays.* OPPOSITE: *Fresh greens and Staffordshire toby mugs spark up a collection of antique pewter.*

All of the decorating materials are fresh and from the surrounding countryside. Linda dries apple and orange slices to include in wreaths, and the gingerbread-men cookies are made from an applesauce and cinnamon mixture. Fresh apples, pineapples, grapes, and oranges also make their appearance as decoration. And everywhere are facsimiles of Noah's Ark; the Mattes family has a fine collection made by folk artists from all over the United States. Their fondness for this biblical motif prompted them to forgo the conventional gingerbread house in favor of a gingerbread ark complete with gingerbread animals made from their own patterns and painted with royal icing.

Another holiday tradition, candy making, gives Linda an opportunity to use her handsome antique lollipop molds. The finished candies, flavored with spicy essences and wrapped in cellophane, sparkle like jewels, adding yet another festive note to the bustling atmosphere.

ABOVE: *A Santa Claus dressed in a costume of combined antique fiber pieces stands next to a stack of old wooden boxes in one of the bedrooms.* BELOW: *Antique baskets filled with decorating materials crowd the deep windowsills.*

THE STORIES OF CHRISTMAS GREENS

When we bring in armloads of pine, spruce, and holly to bedeck our homes for the holidays, we are enacting traditions that began with the ancient Druids, Romans, and Christians, all of whom believed greens had magical properties. Even primitive people hung holly above doorways to encourage woodland spirits to enter their huts during the winter solstice.

Early Christians believed holly had sprung up from Jesus's footsteps as he walked through the Holy Land preaching the gospel. The ancient Greeks believed ivy brought fruitfulness. (Remember that when you garnish your trays with this lovely small-leafed vine.)

In medieval England, holly and ivy became thought of as Christmas greens, inspiring one of the loveliest carols. According to legend, the first person to bring holly into the house would rule the home in the coming year. Evergreen trees were considered a symbol of eternal life; they showed that no matter how hard the winter, the earth would come back to life in the spring. Fragrant pine and fir boughs were thought to bring good luck, even fertility.

Mistletoe kissing balls were first popular during the Victorian period, but the ancients thought mistletoe was magical. Druids worshiped it, and Roman warriors used it as a symbol of peace. When opponents met beneath the mistletoe, they put down their arms, kissed each other, and declared a truce for the rest of the day. By the Middle Ages, even the most humble of English cottagers were hanging mistletoe in their doorway and kissing beneath it.

Later, frou-frou–loving English Victorians designed kissing balls for the mistletoe, and today in America we hang it in our houses without much thought to either the Victorians or the Druids. Every December, I weave several branches of mistletoe with a handful of dried flowers and attach the arrangement, with greens, to the top of my bed.

BELOW LEFT: *Homemade cookies, with designs drawn and cut out by Linda's mother, Ellen Jaap, decorate the tree, along with sycamore balls, cranberry strands, and kumquats studded with cloves.* BELOW RIGHT: *Amish leather horse reins, intertwined with pine garlands and fresh fruit, wind their way up the staircase. A fresh pineapple, treasured during the Victorian period, is an appropriate punctuation point.*

OPPOSITE AND ABOVE: *Orange slices drying on their screens look like a contemporary painting. Orange slices cut approximately a quarter inch thick will take three to four days to dry. Fruit can also be dried for three or four hours in a gas oven at 150° F., with the oven door left open slightly, or in a dehydrator set at 135° F.* **BELOW LEFT**: *Dried apple and orange slices grace wreaths and, dotted with whole star anise, glow in the sunlight like stained glass*, **BELOW RIGHT**.

APPLESAUCE AND CINNAMON ORNAMENTS

Ornaments made with this simple mixture turn out dark brown and fragrant and stay firm for years. This is really an ideal substitute for ginger cookie ornaments—it takes fewer ingredients and the dough is easier for children (and adults) to work with. And there is no baking! For best results, drain the applesauce overnight in a sieve to remove excess moisture.

MATERIALS/INGREDIENTS

1 1-pound jar sweetened applesauce, drained

8 ounces ground cinnamon, or more if necessary

wax paper or parchment paper

TOOLS/EQUIPMENT

electric mixer and bowl

assorted cookie cutters

match or toothpick

1. In a mixer bowl, gradually combine the applesauce with the ground cinnamon, alternating the ingredients until the mixture reaches the consistency of cookie dough. (Applesauce texture varies because of the water content in the apples themselves, so you have to judge the proper stiffness by the feel of the dough.)

2. Working with about 1 cup of the mixture at a time, pat the dough with your hands onto wax or parchment paper to about ¼ inch thick.

3. Using decorative cookie cutters, cut out ornaments, and with an old-fashioned wooden match or a toothpick, make a hole in the top of each.

4. Dry the ornaments in a warm place for a week, turning them every day.

MAKES 48 3½-INCH ORNAMENTS

Dough made from applesauce and cinnamon is easy to roll and cut into shapes and needs no baking. The dried ornaments can be strung with dried fruit slices, bay leaves, and cinnamon sticks for a festive garland.

GINGERBREAD ARK AND ANIMALS

This is a very firm, dark gingerbread that lends itself well to pattern making and cookie ornaments. Four batches of gingerbread are required to make the ark and animals. This dough can also be used for gingerbread houses.

MATERIALS/INGREDIENTS

½ cup (1 stick) margarine, at room temperature

¾ cup sugar

1 large egg

¼ cup dark molasses

3 tablespoons orange juice

3½–4 cups all-purpose flour

1 teaspoon baking soda

1 teaspoon ground cinnamon

1 teaspoon ground ginger

½ teaspoon salt

wax paper

TOOLS/EQUIPMENT

electric mixer and bowl

large mixing bowl

whisk

cookie sheet

spatula

cooling rack

1. In a large mixer bowl, cream the margarine and sugar until fluffy, about 3 minutes. Add the egg, molasses, and orange juice; beat well. In another large bowl, whisk together the flour, baking soda, cinnamon, ginger, and salt; add gradually to the creamed mixture, blending well.

2. Divide the dough in half and wrap each half in plastic wrap. Chill for 1 hour, or until the dough is firm enough to handle.

3. Preheat the oven to 350° F. On a greased cookie sheet, roll out one portion of the dough to ⅛ inch thick. (Keep the other portion refrigerated until ready to use.) Cut the animal or ark pattern out on the cookie sheet and remove the excess dough with a metal spatula.

4. Bake for 10 minutes, remove the sheet from the oven, and allow the cookies to cool for 1 minute. Remove the cookies to racks lined with wax paper to cool.

MAKES APPROXIMATELY
3 DOZEN COOKIES

GINGERBREAD

We are apt to associate gingerbread cookies and houses with Christmas. However, the tradition of making treats with pungent ginger goes back centuries. Native to China and India, ginger was introduced to the Greeks by Arab traders. The Romans enjoyed it as a cooking ingredient and the Crusaders brought it back to Europe, along with other treasures from the Middle East.

The English used ginger in cookery, too, but it was the fourteenth-century Germans who really took gingerbread seriously—they even formed guilds of gingerbread artisans. They made creations for the aristocracy from elaborately carved molds that were wonders to be-hold. In the seventeenth century, molasses was added, and the peasants and emerging middle class began to make gingerbread to celebrate holidays. When the Brothers Grimm wrote their eighteenth-century tale about Hansel and Gretel, they described a house "made of bread, with a roof of cake and windows of barley." The decorative gingerbread house has been with us ever since.

In the United States, gingerbread has been popular since colonial days, when Salem, Massachusetts, was an important spice-trading center. But it didn't take long for the spice to move westward, and now gingerbread treats are popular across the country.

ROYAL ICING

This basic decorative icing is always used for gingerbread houses because it is so trustworthy; it hardens up beautifully, and since it is plain white, it takes the tinted dyes you will want to use for coloring the trimming or ornaments. Use the intensely colored paste colors available at bakeware and candy-making shops for the most professional-looking results.

Prepacked royal icing mixtures are also available at candy-making shops (see the Directory). These are made simply by adding water.

MATERIALS/INGREDIENTS
1 pound confectioners' sugar
3 large egg whites, at room temperature
½ teaspoon cream of tartar
speck of salt
paper towel or plastic wrap

TOOLS/EQUIPMENT
electric mixer and bowl
pastry bags and tips (optional)
toothpick

1. If the sugar is even slightly lumpy, sift it before using. In a mixer bowl, combine the egg whites, confectioners' sugar, cream of tartar, and salt. Beat on high speed until the icing is stiff enough to hold its shape, adding more sugar if necessary.

2. Cover the mixture with a moist paper towel, or place plastic wrap directly on the surface. Or transfer it directly to pastry bags and cover the tips with plastic wrap. Store any extra icing, covered, in the refrigerator.

3. To tint the icing, use wooden toothpicks to add dots of paste color to the icing until the color you want is achieved. If you are painting cookies with the icing, place a small amount in a custard cup, tint it, then thin with drops of water until it is spreadable with a paintbrush. If it is too thin, add a bit more icing.

MAKES ABOUT 2 CUPS ICING

ABOVE: *When assembled, it's hard to tell which one is the wooden ark and which one is the cookie replica. (The edible one is in the foreground.)* **OPPOSITE**: *A sample of the family's animal patterns.*

CLEAR TOY CANDY

This recipe was devised for use with antique iron candy molds (see Directory for sources), but it can also be used to make lollipops or sugarplums to hang on the tree. It is best to make this candy on a clear, sunny day; if there is too much humidity in the atmosphere, the candy may be cloudy.

It is best to pour and later store the candy in a cool place; I like to work in the garage, but you can certainly do this in the house if you are not cooking other foods that create moisture.

MATERIALS/INGREDIENTS

2 cups granulated cane sugar (don't use beet sugar)

⅔ cup light corn syrup (preferably Karo red label)

⅔ cup water

good-quality olive oil

paper towels

rubber bands

few drops of peppermint, wintergreen, or cinnamon extract

few drops of red or green coloring

wax paper and parchment paper

wooden sticks (optional—for lollipops)

100 8- or 9-inch lengths of plastic fishing line (optional—for sugarplums)

TOOLS/EQUIPMENT

heavy saucepan

candy thermometer

candy molds

screwdriver

cookie sheet (optional)

1. In a heavy saucepan, preferably one with a good pouring lip, combine the sugar, syrup, and water. Cook over medium-low heat, stirring constantly, until the sugar is completely dissolved and you can see that the mixture is getting hot. Insert a candy thermometer, and do not stir after the candy reaches 200° F.

2. Meanwhile, prepare the molds. Brush each liberally with olive oil and turn them upside down for a few minutes on paper towels to drain off any excess oil. Turn them right side up and fasten together with rubber bands. Place them in a row, closely together, so they prop each other up.

3. Cook the candy to 290° F. if it is a clear day, and to 300° F. if it is the least bit humid. (This took nearly 40 minutes on my stove over medium-low heat.) When the candy is within 10° of the desired tempera-

ture, add the flavoring and coloring. Do not stir in—the bubbling of the mixture will do the combining. No color is required for yellow candy.

4. If making molded candies, quickly pour the candy into the molds; the mixture might foam up a bit in the molds, so be careful. Allow the candy to stand for approximately 15 minutes. The candy should not be allowed to cool completely in the molds or you won't be able to get it out. If you take it out too soon, the figures will bend; keep checking them, and you will soon be able to discern when it is time to remove the candy.

5. Remove the rubber bands and, with a screwdriver, pry the molds apart. With a small knife, carefully lift out the candy. The little pieces will be quite firm, the larger pieces a tad soft. For very large molds, such as a ship or train mold, allow the candy to set in the molds for a few minutes longer. Store unwrapped on wax-paper–lined plates.

To make lollipops, arrange wooden sticks (available at hobby and food specialty stores) in rows on parchment-lined or greased cookie sheets. Pour the hot syrup in a thin stream over each stick, forming rounds of candy as large or as small as you like. Let cool.

To make sugarplums for hanging, make loops of the fishing line on parchment-covered or well-greased baking sheets, or in miniature muffin cups. Drop the candy mixture from the tip of a teaspoon over each loop. Let cool.

MAKES ABOUT 10 MOLDED CANDIES, 20 LOLLIPOPS, OR 100 SUGARPLUMS

HARD CANDIES

Nineteenth-century Pennsylvania Dutch children believed the Christ Child, or *Grisch-kindel,* would arrive on a donkey on Christmas Eve to bring them presents. Setting out their dinner plates, off they went to bed. The next morning, the plates would be filled with fresh fruit (an expensive and rare treat at that time), nuts, and molded hard candies, called clear toys. This clear candy is solely a winter confection, for humidity is its enemy—the color becomes murky and the Santas sag.

The ingredients are few, and during the 1800s, barley sugar was used instead of imported cane sugar for reasons of economy, giving the candy the common name "barley pops."

Antique iron molds are collectors' items, and even the reproductions are costly. However, you might want to buy one mold a year and start a collection. Once you make these candies, you'll be enchanted—the molds have great presence and charm. The various shapes range in subject from train engines to birds and animals, and even clasped hands.

The candies really are clear miniature toys, and it is easy to see why the Pennsylvania Dutch children loved receiving them. Later, the term *Grisch-kindel* became the Pennsylvania Dutch expression for a Christmas gift.

George and Linda's social life in December revolves first and foremost around the family; traditionally they all meet on Christmas Eve after church services. The menu is primarily Victorian, in keeping with both the house and many of the dishes and serving accessories. After Christmas, the family hosts an open house for a hundred of their friends, and a similar menu is served.

"I really believe in the Christmas spirit," laughs Linda. "Something very singular happens every year to make it a happy time for us all."

ABOVE: *Tina and Gary fill their plates from the lavish buffet. The Victorian Sherry Jelly and Steamed Persimmon Christmas Pudding on footed stands make handsome centerpieces.*
OPPOSITE: *Clutching the coveted pickle ornament (she had a bit of help in finding it) a tuckered-out Chloe sleeps contentedly in her grandmother's arms.*

VICTORIAN PICKLE CHRISTMAS ORNAMENT

The custom is British Victorian; the tale is medieval Spanish. And it exemplifies how we borrow traditions from all over the world to make Christmas "ours."

Once upon a time in Spain, several young boys were traveling home from boarding school for the Christmas holidays. On the way, they became tired and stopped at an inn for the night. They had no idea the innkeeper was a cruel and wicked man. (This smacks of the Brothers Grimm!) The innkeeper looked the boys over and speculated they would be good to eat. He chopped them up and put them in a pickle barrel.

Along came St. Nicholas and, because he was all-seeing, all-knowing, he knew what had happened to the boys. He touched his bishop's staff to the barrel and the boys became whole again, presumably going on home for Christmas.

From this rather macabre story came the Victorian custom of hiding a pickle-shaped ornament on the Christmas tree; the child who finds it gets an extra gift. Pickle ornaments can be ordered by mail (see the Directory).

A VICTORIAN LEGACY

Queen Victoria and her consort, Prince Albert, are responsible for popularizing the Christmas tree with its decorations and lights. Prince Albert had brought the custom with him to England from his own home in Saxe-Coburg, Germany, though historians confirm that Victoria's grandmother had a Christmas tree as early as 1780—a "yew tree placed in an immense tub, from the branches of which hung bunches of sweetmeats, almonds, fruits, toys, and the entire arrangement was illuminated by small wax candles."

However, it was the widely publicized image of Victoria and her brood of children, after the 1840s, along with Dickens's *A Christmas Carol,* with its emphasis on the redeeming strength of a unified and loving family unit, that prompted the rest of England to adopt these royal traditions as their own. American hostesses watched the Queen and her court with fascination, and she very much influenced social customs in our own country, although it was early German immigrants who first brought the Christmas tree (Dickens dubbed it "the new German toy") to the United States.

TOP: *George and Linda Mattes relax over a cup of Syllabub.* RIGHT: *The dining room table has an eye-catching centerpiece—an antique epergne of silver and glass filled with apples and topped with a pineapple. The tureen is ironstone, circa 1850.*

CHRISTMAS EVE SUPPER

Syllabub   Victorian Spiced Nuts

Creamy Oyster Bisque

Hot Biscuits with Honey-Baked Ham

Spicy Rhubarb Chutney

Anglican Mincemeat Tarts

Steamed Persimmon Christmas Pudding
with Nutmeg Hard Sauce

Victorian Sherry Jelly with
Orange and Brandy

Candied Orange Peel

Strawberry Heart Cookies

VICTORIAN SPICED NUTS

To end a very fine meal, American hostesses of the Victorian period would serve salted and spiced nuts in place of the heavier savories of England. The Mattes family serves them with Syllabub.

This recipe has an unexpected bite of curry and chili that makes it very different. The nuts fall into a sweetmeat category, but they are good with cocktails and, packed in antique jars and tied with Christmas ribbon, also make ideal gifts.

You will need a candy thermometer.

½ cup water
1 cup firmly packed brown sugar
1 tablespoon curry powder
1 teaspoon chili powder
¾ teaspoon salt
½ teaspoon white pepper
1 pound toasted English walnuts (see Note)

Oil a large cookie sheet and set aside. In a heavy, medium saucepan, combine all ingredients but the walnuts. Cover and bring to a boil over high heat. (The steam dissolves the sugar crystals on the sides of the pan, keeping the mixture from "going to sugar.") Remove the lid, insert a candy thermometer, and continue boiling until the mixture reaches 260° F. (hard ball). Remove from the heat and immediately add the nuts and stir until well coated.

Quickly transfer the hot mixture to the cookie sheet and separate the nuts into small clumps while they are still warm. Allow them to cool completely and store in an airtight tin.

Note: Toast the unsalted raw walnuts on a cookie sheet in a 300° F. oven for 5 to 10 minutes, or until the nuts begin to turn color. Watch them closely and turn occasionally with a spatula.

MAKES ABOUT 3 CUPS

A collection of glass basket vases are ideal containers for sweetmeats—candied fruits and nuts.

SYLLABUB

*An utterly beguiling punch, this seventeenth-century recipe luckily has never really dropped out of sight—or from cookbooks. It is too delicious to be forgotten. The name is derived from two words—*sillery*, at one time the best-known wine in England, and* bub*, an Elizabethan colloquial name for a bubbling drink.*

Syllabub could be called a cider eggnog. The Victorians served it often; sometimes Madeira or sherry was used in place of all or part of the cider. It is also said that farmers would take pails of cider directly to the barn and milk the cow right into the pails, giving the drink its head of creamy froth.

Make this a day in advance, if you like. Especially if you must arrange for the cow. . . .

½ cup milk
½ cup sugar
2½ cups fresh apple cider
1 teaspoon vanilla extract
speck of salt
2 cups heavy cream
freshly grated nutmeg, for garnish

In a large mixer bowl, combine the milk, sugar, cider, vanilla, and salt. In another bowl, whip the cream until stiff; fold the whipped cream into the cider mixture, then whisk until the syllabub is frothy and completely combined. (It can be stored in the refrigerator at this point; whisk again to recombine before serving.) Serve in punch cups and garnish with grated nutmeg.

MAKES 10 3-OUNCE SERVINGS

CREAMY OYSTER BISQUE

This elegant oyster bisque, a popular Victorian dish with its touch of sherry, is rich and colorful. Celery and onions add additional flavor and texture. The recipe is dated 1865; the Tabasco and vegetable seasoning are optional twentieth-century additions.

4 cups shucked stewing oysters (standards; 32 ounces), undrained

2 celery ribs, chopped into ¼-inch dice

2 medium onions, chopped into ¼-inch dice

½ cup (1 stick) unsalted butter

4 tablespoons all-purpose flour

½ teaspoon salt

¼ teaspoon freshly ground white pepper

½ teaspoon powdered vegetable seasoning

2 cups half-and-half

3 dashes Tabasco sauce (optional)

¼ cup dry sherry

finely minced fresh parsley, for garnish

Drain the oyster liquid into a measuring cup and add enough water to the drained liquid to make 2 cups. Transfer to a large saucepan and add 6 additional cups of water. Chop the oysters coarsely into halves or thirds and reserve. Add half the celery and onions to the oyster liquid and simmer uncovered for 30 minutes, skimming occasionally.

Combine the butter, remaining celery, and onions in a large soup pot and sauté over medium-low heat for about 5 minutes—do not allow the mixture to brown. In a small dish, combine the flour, salt, pepper, and vegetable seasoning; add to the butter-onion mixture and cook 1 minute longer, or until the mixture bubbles up in the center of the pan. Add the oyster broth all at once, whisking smooth, then cook over low heat for 10 minutes. Add the oysters, half-and-half, and Tabasco. Bring to a simmer and cook 2 to 3 minutes. Add the sherry just before serving, and garnish with fresh parsley.

MAKES 8 SERVINGS

HOT BISCUITS

These biscuits rise satisfyingly high. To serve, slice the baked biscuits in half, butter, and fill with slivers of Honey-Baked Ham. These can be made, buttered, and frozen in advance.

3 cups all-purpose flour

2 tablespoons baking powder

2 tablespoons sugar

1 teaspoon salt

1 teaspoon cream of tartar

¼ teaspoon cayenne pepper

½ cup solid vegetable shortening

½ cup (1 stick) cold unsalted butter, cut into chunks

1 to 1½ cups buttermilk, at room temperature

Preheat the oven to 375° F. In a food processor, combine the flour, baking powder, sugar, salt, cream of tartar, and cayenne pepper. Add the shortening and butter and pulse until the mixture forms coarse crumbs. Add 1 cup of the buttermilk and pulse until a firm dough forms —you want to be able to roll it out. Add a bit more buttermilk if the dough is too thick.

Tip the dough out onto a lightly floured surface and, with floured hands, knead it lightly 8 to 10 times, or until smooth. Roll the dough out to a ½-inch-thick patty. Using a 2- or 3-inch biscuit cutter, cut the dough into rounds. Insert the cutter straight down into the dough, and then pull it straight back up—do not move the cutter in a circular pattern as you cut, since this will cause the edges of the biscuit to cling together and the biscuit will tip as it bakes, instead of rising straight up.

Transfer the biscuits to a lightly greased cookie sheet, 2 inches apart, and bake for 13 to 15 minutes, or until golden brown.

MAKES ABOUT 15 3-INCH BISCUITS

SPICY RHUBARB CHUTNEY

A jar of this snappy chutney combining rhubarb, raisins, onions, and lots of spices makes a very nice gift. Serve it with baked ham or roast turkey as a zesty condiment. The recipe dates back to the late 1800s.

2 quarts fresh or frozen chopped rhubarb

1 cup chopped onion

1½ cups chopped seedless raisins

3½ cups firmly packed light brown sugar

½ cup cider vinegar

2 tablespoons mustard seeds

1¼ teaspoons salt

1 teaspoon hot red pepper flakes

1 teaspoon ground cinnamon

1 teaspoon ground ginger

1 teaspoon curry powder

1 teaspoon ground allspice

¼ teaspoon turmeric

red food coloring (optional)

In a deep saucepan, combine the rhubarb, onion, raisins, brown sugar, and vinegar. Bring to a boil over medium heat, then reduce the heat and simmer until thick, about 25 minutes, stirring frequently to prevent sticking. Add the spices; cook 5 minutes longer. Add a few drops of red food coloring, if desired.

Pour, boiling hot, into hot pint jars, leaving ¼-inch head space. With a wet paper towel, wipe off the tops of the jars. Top with the caps and rings, and place in a deep kettle of boiling water, completely covering the tops of the jars by 2 inches. Process for 10 minutes, counting the time after the water comes again to a boil. Remove from the water bath and place on a towel-covered wire rack. Allow to cool and store in a dark place.

Note: If the finished cooled chutney is too thick, thin it to the proper consistency with hot water or corn syrup. The chutney can also be frozen.

MAKES ABOUT 4 PINTS

VICTORIAN SHERRY JELLY WITH ORANGE AND BRANDY

This is a delectable amber-colored whimsy with an intense sherry flavor. Wine jellies, beloved Victorian desserts, were presented in either towering molds or elegant individual dessert glasses. After a sumptuous meal, when the men retired to a separate room for their brandy and cigars, the women would congregate in the parlor and wine jelly would be served. It was a genteel way for the ladies to have a drink after dinner. Today it is a nice addition to a dessert buffet.

2 envelopes unflavored gelatin

2 cups cold water

1 cup sugar

1½ teaspoons grated lemon zest

1 cup sweet dessert sherry

3 tablespoons fresh lemon juice

¼ cup fresh orange juice

2 tablespoons brandy

sweetened whipped cream, for topping (optional)

In a small bowl, sprinkle the gelatin over 1 cup of the water and blend with a fork to dissolve. In a medium saucepan over medium-high heat, combine the remaining 1 cup of water, sugar, and lemon zest and bring to a boil; add the gelatin mixture and simmer about 30 seconds. Remove from the heat and add the sherry, lemon juice, orange juice, and brandy. Pour into a 5-cup decorative mold that has been coated with vegetable cooking spray and refrigerate overnight, or until the mixture has set. Unmold and serve with sweetened whipped cream, if desired.

MAKES 8 SERVINGS

This jellied dessert can be made in various shapes and sizes. The unmolded jelly, arranged on a silver platter and garnished with greenery, is a lovely translucent color.

ANGLICAN MINCEMEAT TARTS

Mincemeat used to be made at butchering time in the late fall as a way to utilize the last scraps of meat. It was simmered very slowly at the back of the fire in a huge iron kettle, and then was stored in crocks on the back porch or in the smokehouse for use all winter long. The preparation was complex and took days. The easier twentieth-century method is to bake the mixture in a heavy roaster in a slow oven. Cook the meat and boil down the cider a day in advance. This recipe makes four quarts of sprightly and fruity mincemeat, enough for four pies or four batches of tarts.

Though we think of tarts as being open faced, this version resembles a very stylish turnover.

MINCEMEAT
4 pounds beef shank, cross cut
1 gallon fresh apple cider
8 pounds apples, peeled and cored (approximately 26 medium apples)
2 pounds light brown sugar, packed
1 pound raisins (3 cups)
1 pound currants (3 cups)
8 ounces candied fruits (1 cup)
1 cup cream sherry
1 cup slivered almonds
½ cup diced citron
2 tablespoons ground cinnamon
2 tablespoons ground cloves
2 tablespoons grated nutmeg
2 teaspoons salt

TARTS
Holiday Pastry (recipe follows), chilled
1 large egg
1 tablespoon water
granulated sugar
red and green candied cherries (optional)

Simmer the shank in water to cover until the meat is very tender, about 1½ hours, or cook in a pressure cooker with 3 cups of water for 30 minutes at the "cook" position. Allow the meat to cool and discard the bones and gristle, reserving the cooking liquid. Transfer the meat to a food processor and pulse until the meat is coarsely minced. Cover the meat and broth separately and refrigerate.

While the meat cooks, boil the cider uncovered in a large kettle over medium-high heat until reduced by half—this takes about 1 hour. Cool and refrigerate.

The next day (or after the meat, broth, and cider have cooled), preheat the oven to 450° F. Finely chop the apples in the food processor and place in a large, heavy roaster with the reserved meat and cider and the remaining ingredients. Combine well, cover, and bake for 45 minutes, then lower the heat to 300° F. and bake 1½ hours longer. Uncover and bake 30 minutes more—the mixture should be moist but not soupy. Cool to room temperature.

To make tarts, preheat the oven to 350° F. Roll out half the chilled pastry dough (keep the rest refrigerated) ⅛ inch thick on a lightly floured board. Cut out the tarts using a 4-inch round cookie cutter. Place a heaping tablespoon of mincemeat on one side and fold the other side over. Crimp the edges with a fork and place on a lightly greased baking sheet. Repeat with the remaining dough.

Beat the egg and water together; brush the tops of the tarts with the mixture, covering them completely, then sprinkle the tops liberally with sugar. Bake for 15 to 20 minutes, or until the tarts are a deep golden color. Remove immediately from the baking sheet and cool. Serve at room temperature or reheat slightly in a microwave. Garnish with red and green candied cherries, if desired.

Note: The mincemeat can be frozen in 1-quart containers; it will keep indefinitely.

MAKES 30 TARTS

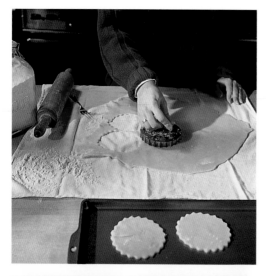

Holiday Pastry

This is a flavorful golden pastry, made with an electric mixer. It is for the cook who has always been apprehensive about making pie crust, for it handles beautifully; make a double recipe and freeze the extra.

4 cups all-purpose flour

1 tablespoon sugar

2 teaspoons salt

1¾ cups butter-flavored solid vegetable shortening

1 large egg

1 tablespoon cider vinegar

½ cup water

Place the dry ingredients and shortening in a large mixer bowl and blend until it has the texture of coarse crumbs. In a small bowl, beat together the egg, vinegar, and water. Drizzle over the flour mixture and mix thoroughly. Shape the dough into a 6-inch patty, wrap in plastic wrap, and place in the freezer for 45 minutes, or refrigerate overnight.

To prepare the dough for pies, form it into a long roll, divide into fourths, and wrap each portion separately and refrigerate or freeze.

MAKES ENOUGH FOR 2 PIES
WITH TOP CRUSTS

STEAMED PERSIMMON CHRISTMAS PUDDING WITH NUTMEG HARD SAUCE

When one thinks of regional Indiana food, one thinks of native American persimmons, which grow in the southern part of the state. The fruits are small, about an inch in diameter, and are harvested in the fall. The most efficient way to gather them is to spread a large sheet under a tree and shake the branches, causing the almost-ripe fruit to fall. The persimmons are then kept in a warm room to finish ripening; the pulp can be either frozen or canned. Persimmon puree can be ordered by mail as can the special mold (see the Directory).

This heavenly dessert is quite marvelous any time of the year, but it is especially appropriate during the holiday season. Serve it with hard sauce.

1 cup sweetened canned persimmon puree

2 teaspoons baking soda

½ cup (1 stick) unsalted butter, at room temperature

½ cup sugar

2 large eggs

2 tablespoons dark rum

1 tablespoon fresh lemon juice

1 cup all-purpose flour

1 teaspoon ground cinnamon

½ teaspoon salt

⅔ cup chopped pecans

Nutmeg Hard Sauce (recipe follows)

Combine the persimmon puree and the baking soda in a small bowl; set aside. In a mixer bowl, cream the butter and sugar for 3 minutes. Add the eggs, blending well after each addition. Quickly mix in the persimmon and the remaining ingredients, except the hard sauce. Do not overbeat.

Grease and flour a 2-quart pudding mold and spoon the batter into it. Cover the mold with its lid or aluminum foil and set on a rack inside a large saucepan or kettle. Add enough water to come halfway up the sides of the mold. Bring to a boil, lower the heat, and steam the pudding, maintaining a gentle simmer for 2 hours, replenishing with boiling water if needed. Remove the pudding from the mold and serve hot with hard sauce.

MAKES 12 SERVINGS

Nutmeg Hard Sauce

This very necessary companion to steamed pudding can be made several days in advance and refrigerated.

½ cup (1 stick) unsalted butter, at room temperature
2 cups confectioners' sugar
3 tablespoons light rum
½ teaspoon grated nutmeg
speck of salt

In large mixer bowl, beat the butter to soften. Add the sugar gradually, then add the rum, nutmeg, and salt and beat until fluffy. Cover and refrigerate. Bring to room temperature before serving.

MAKES 1¼ CUPS SAUCE

Variation: Calvados Hard Sauce

Substitute 3 tablespoons Calvados or applejack for the rum.

CHRISTMAS PUDDING

Christmas pudding. Plum pudding. Suet pudding. The terms are frequently used interchangeably, though they mean different things to different people. The image of the dish was certainly enhanced by Dickens's enthusiastic and loving description in *A Christmas Carol:*

> Hallo! A great deal of steam! The pudding was out of the copper. . . . In half a minute Mrs. Cratchit entered—flushed but smiling proudly—with the pudding, like a speckled cannon ball, so hard and firm, blazing in half of half-quartern of ignited brandy, and bedight with Christmas holly stuck in the top.

Food historians trace the origins of plum pudding to frumenty, a thick porridge of hulled wheat spiced and boiled in milk that was a permitted fasting dish on Christmas Eve. Fruits were eventually added, then meat and suet; soon enough it was on its way to the traditional pudding we know today.

Another version of the pudding story is that one of the medieval English kings was out hunting on Christmas Eve and was unable to get back to the castle. His accompanying cook made up a concoction of frumenty, game, and dried apples. He boiled it in a bag and presented it to his sovereign as a special gift, a nice gesture, indeed.

Dried prunes have been a pudding ingredient through the years and gave rise to the name plum pudding. They are seldom used now; raisins have taken their place.

Ground suet (kidney suet is most prized for its pureness and melting quality) is still an important ingredient, I think, for it gives the pudding a richness and unctuousness that cannot be achieved any other way.

Victorian puddings like those described by Dickens were steamed in cloth pudding bags. My introduction to steamed puddings was one that had been steamed in a special pillowcase kept just for preparing this glorious holiday delicacy. Some cooks have used crockery pudding bowls, and some have used ceramic molds or tins, and still do—the container is probably a matter of tradition in each cook's family or region. See Directory for mail order sources for lidded pudding tins.

CANDIED ORANGE PEEL

Sweetmeats were candies, or sugar-coated fruits and nuts, that appeared on Victorian party tables. For a distinctly non-Victorian flavor treat, add ⅓ cup of this minced peel to your favorite brownie recipe.

4 large navel oranges
3 cups sugar
½ cup water
speck of salt

Slice off the stem end of the oranges. With a sharp knife, lightly score the skins into 6 sections and carefully peel off. Reserve the oranges for another use.

Place the peel in a large deep saucepan and cover with cold water. Bring to a boil and simmer, uncovered, over medium-low heat for 10 minutes. Drain.

Cut the softened rind into ¼-inch strips. Combine 1 cup of the sugar, the water, and the salt in a deep saucepan and boil the mixture until it reaches the coarse-thread stage, 230°–234° F. Add the orange strips to the syrup and stir very gently to mix. Continue cooking 15 minutes longer; the peel will become translucent. Remove from the heat and cool to luke-warm. Gently (the strips are quite tender at this stage) arrange the strips on a rack placed over wax paper or a tray to drain off excess syrup. Let stand for 1 hour.

Place the remaining 2 cups sugar in a shallow pan and roll the cooled strips in the sugar, 5 or 6 at a time, until all the slices are covered. Remove to wax paper and allow to dry thoroughly—about 6 hours.

Store the candied rind in single layers, separated by wax paper, in an airtight container, checking occasionally to see that the rind has not absorbed moisture and softened. If it has, set the lid ajar for a day or two. This has a great deal to do with the humidity, the density of the orange peel, and all those other variables that drive cooks insane. Once completely dried, however, the rind will keep for a month.

MAKES 60 TO 80 PIECES

STRAWBERRY HEART COOKIES

This is a most attractive heart-shaped two-layered cookie, with a very delicate, crisp almond-flavored base and just a smidgen of strawberry jam in the middle. They freeze well, but dust them with confectioners' sugar just before serving.

1½ cups (3 sticks) unsalted butter, softened
1¾ cups confectioners' sugar
1 large egg
1 teaspoon vanilla extract
½ teaspoon grated lemon zest
2 cups all-purpose flour
1 cup cornstarch
1 teaspoon salt
2 cups blanched almonds, ground to a coarse meal
½ cup strawberry jam

In a mixer bowl, cream the butter and 1 cup of the confectioners' sugar until light, about 3 minutes. Add the egg, vanilla, and lemon zest and mix well. In another bowl, whisk together the flour, cornstarch, and salt and add to the creamed mixture. Mix in the ground almonds; you may have to work in the last of them by hand. Wrap the dough in plastic and chill in the refrigerator overnight.

Remove the dough from the refrigerator to

soften slightly about 1 hour before rolling out. Flour a cloth or board lightly, and roll out the dough one-third at a time to ¼ inch thick. (Placing a sheet of wax paper on top of the dough makes it easier to roll.) Cut out an equal number of 1½-inch hearts and 3-inch hearts. Place separately on 2 parchment-lined or un-greased cookie sheets and chill for 45 minutes. Preheat the oven to 325° F.

When chilled, bake the large hearts for 10 minutes and the little hearts for 8 minutes; they should not brown. Let the cookies stand on the pans for 2 minutes and then transfer them to a cooling rack. Immediately, while the cookies are still warm, place about ¼ teaspoon of jam in the center of each 3-inch heart, then top with a smaller heart—you want a bit of the red jam to show. Cool completely, then store in tins or freeze. Just before serving, sift the remaining ¾ cup confectioners' sugar over the tops.

MAKES 3 DOZEN COOKIES

Christmas at Home
with Friends

I love the country and write frequently about it—its landscape, its people, and its food —so it comes as a surprise to most people to discover that I live in a house that is not "country" at all, nor is it filled with antiques and quilts but rather a contemporary art collection. Ours is a glass house, built in the shape of a fan and located about twenty feet from a lakeshore. From the windows, we see the lake and many trees; where there is open space and light, my husband and I have planted deep old-fashioned perennial borders, since we both garden with a passion. Many of the flowers we dry for

FORCING BRANCHES

It is an old German custom to bring in cherry branches on St. Barbara's Day, December 4, so boughs will bloom by Christmas Day. To be assured of success and have the blooms fully out, I prefer to do it right after Thanksgiving. To make sure water goes quickly up into the branches, use a hammer to thoroughly smash the bottom six inches of the branches. Then immerse the branches entirely in a deep sink or tub (I use the bathtub) of warm water overnight; this softens the buds. Arrange the boughs in deep vases and mist them daily.

ABOVE: *Visiting nephews Eric, Josh, and Ryan help Dick cut the long tree branches that will form the backbones of all the interior decorations, while I bed down the herb garden for winter with fresh Christmas tree branches,* OPPOSITE.

winter use, including Christmas decorations. Feeding the birds year-round adds color to the landscape, and wildlife from the nearby woods traverse our property regularly.

At Christmas, we try to bring all these elements from the outside in, duplicating the naturalness of what we see from our windows: decorations using our own dried flowers and herbs, such as PeeGee hydrangeas, red bamboo, Queen Anne's lace, lady's mantle, lamb's ears, globe-amaranth, rosemary, and thyme—the list goes on and on. The fresh flowers are ones we force from bulbs that appear in our garden in the spring—lily of the valley, narcissus, and for good measure, lots of Christmas amaryllis. And we force branches of apple and cherry (an old German custom), which yield miniature blooms. It is a natural, uncontrived way to do the house for the holidays, and one we have come to prefer over the years. For us, Christmas has a bit of the look of spring, truly signaling the end of the winter solstice, one of the holiday's obscure beginnings. I love to find those links to the past!

The crafts that I do at Christmastime tend to be like my favorite recipes—simple and quick, using indigenous ingredients that are readily available. Potpourri, lovingly made over the summer, is used to fill clear glass balls—they are so pretty on the tree and make perfect little hostess gifts. Cranberries and apples, perfection in themselves, look stylish arranged in favorite bowls collected over the years. And of course, we don't forget the birds that add so much to our landscape. They deserve a Christmas treat as well.

In the meantime, I gradually assemble foodstuffs, including a ham or fresh turkey, plus toys if there are children, and fill a large box to be delivered to a needy family before Christmas. My mother always did this; it is important to remember those personal ways to help during a season that is, indeed, all about helping.

120

ABOVE LEFT: *An Advent wreath made of gathered wild things is touched up with a few sycamore balls and a glue gun.* **ABOVE RIGHT**: *Long cinnamon sticks, bay leaf–covered balls, and slices of dried tomatoes fill a handled basket. Nearby, a wooden Amish bread bowl brims with antique apple varieties.*

GOURMET BIRD WREATHS

These make attractive gifts—not only for the birds but for bird lovers. Hang the wreaths on the side of a tree, where they will soon attract woodpeckers and chickadees. You can find straw wreaths at crafts stores.

MATERIALS/INGREDIENTS
2 cups (1 pound) ground kidney suet
½ cup peanut butter
1 cup cornmeal
3 6½-inch straw wreaths
2 cups seed mixture for small birds
3 yards decorative ribbon
12 or 15 grain branches

TOOLS/EQUIPMENT
sauté pan
metal tongs
large metal spoon
9 x 13-inch pan
1 or 2 wax-paper–lined cookie sheets

1. In a large sauté pan, heat the suet over medium-low heat until completely melted. Stir in the peanut butter and cornmeal. (It may be necessary to add a bit more cornmeal if the mixture is too runny—this will depend somewhat on the brand of peanut butter you are using.) Remove from the heat and, with tongs, dip in one of the wreaths, covering the entire surface with the suet mixture. Use a spoon to coat the inside.

2. Place the bird seed in the pan and roll the warm suet-covered wreath in the seed, completely covering the wreath, patting the seed on if necessary. Place on the cookie sheet. Repeat with the remaining wreaths. If the suet mixture begins to harden, reheat it slightly and continue dipping.

3. Refrigerate the wreaths overnight. Tie with bows and decorate with grain branches.

MAKES 3 WREATHS

BIRD CHRISTMAS TREATS

The river birch right outside our front door has a handsome shape even in winter. It seemed a perfect place for a Bird Christmas Treats tree, but we wanted it also to be visually decorative. These little bird baskets were the perfect solution—and we had many, many different kinds of birds for nearly two months.

MATERIALS/INGREDIENTS

8 pounds ground kidney suet

1½ cups peanut butter

6–8 cups cornmeal

10 cups good-quality bird seed

100 paper muffin liners

50 3-inch wicker baskets with handles (available at crafts shops)

50 cranberries

15 yards red twine

TOOLS/EQUIPMENT

saucepan

large mixing bowls

whisk

tablespoon

1. Melt the suet in a deep pan over low heat, about 45 to 60 minutes. Divide between 2 large bowls, add ¾ cup of peanut butter to each, and whisk in. Then add the cornmeal, starting with just 3 cups in each bowl. Stir half the bird seed into each. If the mixture is too soft, add more cornmeal. Chill overnight in the refrigerator or garage.

2. Place double muffin liners (don't use foil— the reflection will frighten the birds) in each basket. Leave the suet mixture at room temperature until it is soft enough to scoop out with a tablespoon. Heap the baskets with suet mixture, about ½ cup in each basket. Top each with a fresh cranberry. (Place any leftover suet mixture in a mesh potato or onion bag and tie it to a tree.)

ABOVE: *Dick hangs bird baskets on a river birch tree. They will be emptied by enthusiastic feathered guests by Valentine's Day, when they will be refilled.*
OPPOSITE: *Large straw wreaths covered with seeds and decorated are another bird favorite.*

3. Using 10-inch lengths of red twine, tie the baskets to tree branches. It might take a couple of days for the birds to discover their gift, but discover it they will.

MAKES 50 BIRD TREATS

CHRISTMAS GIFT WRAPPING

I don't know when it began, but for years I have used nothing but solid red paper for wrapping all our Christmas gifts. The paper comes in long rolls, so I buy several boxes plus transparent tape, lots of wide and narrow white ribbon, and start wrapping gifts in early November; my goal is to do about five presents a night while I am watching television. The drama of one color under the tree pleases my eye and certainly simplifies decision making. And it is probably more economical as well.

For package decorations, I use old Christmas cards. Some must be twenty years old and are simply too beautiful to throw away; the three-dimensional ones are extraordinarily handsome, and one on a box is often all the decoration the present needs. The recipients of those packages are always cautioned: "Be careful of the card, so I can use it again."

I also add dried flowers such as statice, lavender, globe amaranth, and *Nepata Mussinii* to the packages, though the cats, Emily and Edith, like nibbling the posies. Queen Anne's lace is a particular favorite of mine, year-round, but very fragile; I place dried nosegays of it in heavy paper baskets and then attach a basket to each package.

Here is how to dry Queen Anne's lace: when it blooms in July, pick it early in the morning and leave the long stems attached. Insert the stems through a coarse upturned sieve suspended on shoe boxes or bricks, or through flat pieces of chicken wire, with the head of the flower suspended on the top of the sieve or wire. Lay a piece of wax paper on top of the flower head so it won't curl up. Allow to dry thoroughly for one week. Spray with hair spray and store until needed in long boxes lined with tissue paper.

OPPOSITE: *Candles glow in a variety of ceramic Mexican candleholders.*

My nieces, left to right, *Jessica, Sarah, and Samantha, decorate the little tree in my study, using fresh-popped corn, lady apples, and old toys.*

I admit I am childishly delighted when, on the first weekend in December, we begin unpacking the decorations. That very weekend, decorating begins in earnest. On Saturday, the crèches (we have collected quite a number) are set out; the Advent wreath of cones, seed pods, and nuts—lovingly constructed more than twenty years ago with our two children from material we had gathered all over the country—is filled with candles; and the Christmas tree ornaments, all individually wrapped, are unpacked and laid carefully on large trays. The next day, Sunday, we hang them all, each one eliciting a memory of a time or person. I chuckle when I tell people that I have cataloged every ornament—it sounds so compulsive. Yet it is not a reflection of the ornament's monetary value, but rather its sentimental value. I want to recall the day and place we bought each one and relive the experience year after year.

Christmas is also the time I yield to red ribbons and Teddy bears, bringing out favored old china and toys from childhood. Calling on nieces and nephews to help (I like having the children around and this is such a *good* excuse!), we cut tree branches in the woods, bring in the pre-planted pots of paperwhite narcissus and lily-of-the-valley to force, make suet wreaths for the birds, and string popcorn strands for the mini-tree in the study. As an exhilaratingly messy treat, the children make homemade Christmas cards and star ornaments to take home.

CHRISTMAS STARS

This project is simplicity itself. The finished stars are perfect to hang on the tree or in the window, or even to decorate gifts. I have also used them as napkin rings and party favors at Christmas luncheons. I asked my nieces to make these, and they pronounced the assignment "really neat."

MATERIALS
wide black marker pen
star cookie cutter
shirt cardboards
wax paper
craft glue
assorted colors of glitter
transparent fishing line or thin ribbon

TOOLS/EQUIPMENT
stapler
scissors

1. With the marker pen, mark around the cookie cutter star to make a template on the cardboards. I made 3 stars on each board, arranging them down the center of the cardboard. Cover each shirt board with wax paper, stapling it into place. Using the bottle of glue with its tip on, trace the star shapes onto the wax paper, with thick, ½-inch-wide lines of glue.

2. Using one color of glitter per board, immediately sprinkle a lavish amount of glitter onto each glue star so it is completely covered. Allow to dry for 2 days.

3. Shake off the excess glitter into saucers, to be reused. Cut away the excess wax paper, then carefully peel the glitter stars away from the backing. The stars can be used at this stage for package decorations. However, they will be stronger and more attractive if you place them on a wax-paper–lined cookie sheet, squeeze more glue on the un-glittered side, and sprinkle on more glitter. Allow to dry for 2 more days.

4. Using transparent fishing line or thin ribbon, hang the stars from the tree or in a window, or attach to packages.

INDIANA HYDRANGEA BALLS

A group of these heaped in a shallow silver bowl intertwined with pale pink and green ribbon is a pretty sight and even makes a quick centerpiece when fresh flowers aren't available. Hung from narrow ribbons attached with florist's pins, hydrangea balls can also be used for tree decorations.

MATERIALS
6 dried pink or green PeeGee hydrangea
  blooms
6 2½-inch Styrofoam balls
Styrofoam block, approximately 3 x 5 inches

TOOLS/EQUIPMENT
manicure scissors
metal skewers
hot glue gun
tweezers
small bowl of ice water

1. With the manicure scissors, snip off individual 4-petaled flowerets from the hydrangea blooms and set aside. Insert a metal skewer through one of the balls and stand the skewer upright in the Styrofoam block.

2. With the glue gun, coat a ¼- to ½-inch patch on the ball. Using the tweezers, quickly place a hydrangea floweret on the hot glue, tapping it in with the tweezers. (These flowerets can be put on upside down and the tiny stems trimmed away when the ball is completed.)

3. If you get any glue on your fingers—a likely proposition—immerse your fingers in the ice water. Continue applying glue and flowerets until the ball is completely covered. When the balls are completed, remove the skewers and arrange in a shallow basket or silver bowl.

MAKES 6 HYDRANGEA BALLS

HOLIDAY TOPIARIES

The topiary shape is a pleasing one that has been used for centuries as a decorative motif. At holiday time, topiaries are easily made from dried pomegranates, which are costly but will last for years, or from fresh cranberries, an economical substitute that won't last more than a week. Dried pomegranates may be a bit hard to find; you can order them from your florist or by mail (see the Directory). I make my topiaries in clay pots and set them in a decorative bowl or vase.

MATERIALS
plaster of Paris
1 (4-inch) clay pot
1 sturdy branch, approximately 1½ inches in diameter
1 (4-inch) green Styrofoam ball
white craft glue
clear liquid floor wax
50 (3-inch) wooden florist's picks
50 small dried pomegranates, *or* 1 (16-ounce) bag cranberries
boxwood or arborvitae sprigs
wild rose hips or chinaberries

TOOLS/EQUIPMENT
sharp knife
hot glue gun
electric drill with small bit

1. Mix up about 2 cups of plaster of Paris according to directions. Fill the clay pot and center the branch in the pot. Allow the plaster to harden completely, preferably overnight.

2. With a sharp knife, cut a hole in the Styrofoam ball to fit the top of the branch snugly. Coat the branch top generously with glue, place the ball on top, and allow the glue to dry completely.

3. If using pomegranates, place them on newspaper and spray or brush on liquid wax; allow to dry. Drill a small hole in the bottom of each pomegranate opposite the stem end and insert a florist's pick.

4. Starting at the bottom, cover the ball completely with your chosen material, inserting pomegranates directly into the foam and attaching cranberries with the hot glue gun. Place the material as close together as pos-

sible, working around the ball as you go. Fill in any empty spots with greenery and add clumps of rose hips or berries for accent, holding them in place with hot glue if needed.

MAKES 1 TOPIARY

OPPOSITE: *Mistletoe, greens, and narrow ribbons festoon the brass bed in our bedroom.* ABOVE: *The unicorn, a garden sculpture created by a friend, reclines among white tulips, hyacinths, and branches of forced apple blossoms.* BELOW LEFT: *My own Indiana version of a* putz—*the rosewood figures are from the original Bethlehem. The driftwood, washed up on the lakeshore near our house, is put to good use as a background for the crèche.* BELOW RIGHT: *A pomegranate topiary in Chinese ginger jar.*

Some of our traditions have changed over the years, as our children grew up and moved away, and as we, too, moved farther from our immediate families. The holidays began to be as much about friends as family, widening the circle to include those who are involved in our daily lives.

With our children gone, friends sometimes now join us to help decorate the tree, but we still serve the same menu we had for family—tourtière and Christmas cookies for dessert. If we are having larger parties, then I ask our friends to perform between the soup and entrée from the little gallery that overlooks our living room. My

We celebrate the holidays with our friends the Shultzes sometime during December, exchanging gifts and having a quiet dinner together. Easy-to-make cheese wafers and cocktails, ABOVE, are simple starters; apple sorbet and cookies follow the entrée. The decoration over the fireplace includes wild red bamboo from our garden—it lasts for months after cutting.

HOME FOR CHRISTMAS

This is meeting time again. Home is the magnet. The winter land roars and hums with the eager speed of return journeys. The dark is noisy and bright with late-night arrivals— doors thrown open, running shadows on snow, open arms, kisses, voices and laughter, laughter at everything and nothing. Inarticulate, giddying, and confused are those original minutes of being back again. The very familiarity of everything acts like shock. Contentment has to be drawn in slowly, steadyingly, in deep breaths—there is so much of it. We rely on home not to change, and it does not, wherefore we give thanks. Again Christmas: abiding point of return. Set apart by its mystery, mood, and magic, the season seems in a way to stand outside time. All that is dear, that is lasting, renews its hold on us; we are home again. . . .

This glow of Christmas, has it not in it also the gold of a harvest? "They shall return with joy, bringing their sheaves with them." To the festival, to each other, we bring in wealth. More to tell, more to understand, more to share. Each we have garnered in yet another year; to be glad, to celebrate to the full, we are come together. How akin we are to each other, how speechlessly dear and one in the fundamentals of being, Christmas shows us. No other time grants us, quite, this vision—round the tree or gathered before the fire we perceive anew, with joy, one another's faces. And each time faces come to mean more.

Is it not one of the mysteries of life that life should, after all, be so simple? Yes, as simple as Christmas, simple as this. Journeys through the dark to lighted door, arms open. Laughter-smothered kisses, kiss-smothered laughter. And blessedness in the heart of it all. Here are the verities, all made gay with tinsel. Dear, silly Christmas-card sayings and cracker mottoes— let them speak! Or, since still we cannot speak, let us sing! Dearer than memory, brighter than expectation is the ever returning now of Christmas. Why else, each time we greet its return, should happiness ring out in us like a peal of bells?

Elizabeth Bowen
"Home for Christmas," 1955

affection for "readings" at Christmas goes back to childhood, when my two brothers and I would reenact for the family the whole Nativity drama the night before Christmas.

Many of our friends are involved with the arts, and through the years we have fostered a tradition of reading aloud at some of our parties, picking selections that fit the occasion; we all look forward to it, performers and audience alike. Friends who are fine singers are also pressed into performing. At Christmas, there is lots of good material, and we have never had the same offering twice.

The dinner menu changes each year, but I always end with a dessert buffet—what better time to pull out all the stops? And really, I couldn't pick just *one* dessert! So we have a selection of five to choose from, and people tend to try them all.

Our observance of Christmas in this twentieth-century house is a further affirmation of America's connection to the past—I would have it no other way. By using such old motifs as antique apples to decorate the pine swags and preparing food from "attic receipts," I have a way of sharing these age-old customs in a contemporary setting with my family and friends. Christmas comes together for most of us as a collection of cherished memories tempered by today's realities. Still, the holiday remains a celebration of our unique identities, using a ribbon of memory and family traditions to bind us all as one during Christmas.

Dick helps a guest to some duck from the buffet dinner table; on the sideboard, desserts and coffee are ready and waiting for the guests.

ABOVE: *Judge Dick Ver Wiebe performs before the harpsichord, framed by a swag of greens, antique apples, and PeeGee hydrangea cut and dried in August. Coating the flower heads with hair spray sets the color.* OPPOSITE: *Members of the drama quartette prepare themselves for their presentation.*

CHRISTMAS READINGS

Giving readings or devising playlets is something I've always loved to do, stemming back no doubt to those days when all the children in our neighborhood gathered together (this was before television, remember!) in a deserted carriage house and wrote, produced, and performed our own plays.

Once the play was ready to be performed—this preparation may have taken a couple of weeks—we then fanned out, selling tickets at every door for a nickel each. The money we gathered was not spent on props—those all came from our attics and closets—but instead on wonderfully thick chocolate malts at a local soda shop.

So today it seems natural to me to ask friends to read aloud after dinner. We've done ambitious things, such as excerpts from Shaw's *Man and Superman,* lots of Shakespeare, Robert Frost, Carl Sandburg, Emily Dickinson. . . . One Labor Day, we presented works of American poets, all celebrating the American work ethic. That is probably very Midwestern!

Every reader chooses his or her own material, and especially at Christmas, there is a fine list available. Dickens, of course, is a fantastic source, and in some cases, readings from the Bible are appropriate. Some books we have used are *A Book of Christmas,* by William Sansom (McGraw-Hill, 1968), *Christmas: Penhaligon's Scented Treasury of Verse and Prose,* edited by Sheila Pickles (Harmony Books, 1989), and *May Your Days Be Merry & Bright: Christmas Stories by Women,* edited by Susan Koppelman (New American Library, 1991). If you need more help, ask for assistance at your library.

Dinner in Front of the Fireplace

Cheese Lace Wafers

Tourtière (Canadian Pork Pie)

Green Apple Cider Ice

Orange, Red Onion, and Bibb Lettuce Salad
with Orange Dressing

COOKIE TRAY

Chocolate Noëls, Gingerbread Hearts,
Victorian Scrap Cookies

CHEESE LACE WAFERS

*This delicate cheese wafer is a bit of a surprise—
it has only one ingredient, which should satisfy
even the busiest of cooks. Plain Monterey Jack
cheese can be used, but the added snap of the
jalapeños is something I especially like.*

**1 12-ounce package Monterey Jack cheese
with jalapeños**

Preheat the oven to 350° F. Cut the cheese into
½-inch cubes. Lightly coat a 16 x 13-inch baking sheet with vegetable cooking spray. Place 6
cubes at a time on the sheet, approximately
6 inches apart. Bake for 3 to 5 minutes, watching very carefully. The cheese will melt and
bubble up; when the bubbling stops, the wafer
is done. Remove immediately with a metal
spatula to a rack that has been covered with
paper toweling. When cool, pack in a tightly
covered container.

MAKES APPROXIMATELY 48 WAFERS

*Savory Tourtière, made in advance and frozen,
is ideal for December entertaining. The china is
from M. Dallas Company, and the napkins are
by Vera Bradley.*

TOURTIÈRE (CANADIAN PORK PIE)

Tourtière, or pork pie, is French Canadian in origin and is traditionally eaten on Christmas Eve after Mass. It was first made with passenger pigeons, or tourtes, *as they were known to the Bretons living in Nova Scotia. But the birds, once plentiful, have vanished from the skies—and from the pies as well. When the French Canadians starting migrating into the upper Midwest, they brought the recipe with them, substituting the local pork and beef for bird. It is a savory and sturdy pie that can be made in advance and frozen, and served hot or at room temperature with hot spiced applesauce. The filling is best prepared one day in advance to allow the flavors to marry.*

FILLING

6 tablespoons (¾ stick) unsalted butter

2 pounds coarsely ground round steak (no substitutes)

1 pound very lean ground pork

1 garlic clove, finely minced

1 tablespoon catsup

1 bay leaf

1 teaspoon salt

1 teaspoon dried savory

¾ teaspoon dried thyme

½ teaspoon dry mustard

½ teaspoon ground allspice

½ teaspoon mace

2 medium potatoes, peeled and quartered

15 saltine crackers (don't use cocktail crackers)

paprika, for garnish

½ recipe Holiday Pastry (page 113)

In a deep skillet, melt the butter over medium heat. Add all the filling ingredients except the potatoes and crackers, and cook until the meat is done, about 15 minutes. If the mixture is too juicy (and this will vary, depending on the moisture content of the meat), spoon out some of the juices. It should not be too dry, however.

Meanwhile, boil the potatoes until tender. Mash just enough to make coarse pieces, the size of a pea. Crush or pulse the crackers in a food processor until finely ground. Add potatoes and cracker meal to the meat mixture and combine. If it seems too moist, add a few more crumbs. Remove the bay leaf and set aside to cool for at least 30 minutes, or overnight.

Preheat the oven to 375° F. Roll out the bottom crust and line a 10-inch deep-dish pie pan. Pack the meat mixture firmly into the pie shell, top with the top crust, slash the top in a decorative pattern, and sprinkle with paprika. (The pie can be frozen at this stage—it should be thawed very slowly before baking.) Bake for 1 hour, or until juices bubble up in the center of the pie.

MAKES 8 TO 10 GENEROUS SERVINGS

ORANGE, RED ONION, AND BIBB LETTUCE SALAD WITH ORANGE DRESSING

This is a fine winter salad, tart and fresh, with thinly sliced oranges and mild red onion. The dressing has a hint of orange marmalade, which gives it a nice texture.

3 heads Bibb lettuce

3 small fresh navel oranges, peeled and thinly sliced into rounds

1 medium red onion, thinly sliced and separated into rings

DRESSING

½ cup olive oil

¼ cup rice wine vinegar

2 tablespoons balsamic vinegar

2 tablespoons orange marmalade

¼ teaspoon salt

¼ teaspoon freshly ground black pepper

Arrange the lettuce leaves on a large oval platter. Alternate orange slices and red onion rings in an attractive pattern on top.

Combine the dressing ingredients in a jar and shake well. Drizzle the dressing over the salad; do not toss it.

MAKES 6 SERVINGS

GREEN APPLE CIDER ICE

This refreshing pale green ice is perfect with any pork or poultry dish. Present it in glass, since it is visually attractive, and add a splash of Calvados for good measure.

2 cups apple cider

½ cup water

1½ cups sugar

1⅛ teaspoons anise seed

1 teaspoon ground cinnamon

6 tart apples, such as McIntosh, cored, peeled, and coarsely chopped, about 4 cups

3 tablespoons fresh lemon juice

1 teaspoon grated lemon zest

½ cup Calvados or applejack

speck of salt

few drops green food coloring

additional Calvados or applejack

unpeeled red apple slices, for garnish

In a medium saucepan, boil the cider, uncovered, over medium high heat until reduced to 1 cup, about 20–25 minutes. Add the water, sugar, anise seed, and cinnamon. Bring to a boil and boil over medium heat for 1 minute, or until the sugar dissolves. Remove from the heat, cover, and let cool. Strain through a double thickness of cheesecloth and set aside.

Place the prepared apples in a food processor bowl fitted with a steel blade. Add the lemon juice and zest and puree until very smooth. Add the ½ cup Calvados, salt, food coloring, and the reserved cider mixture and blend.

Pour the mixture into an ice cream maker and freeze according to manufacturer's instructions. Alternatively, pour into a 10 x 10-inch metal baking pan and place in the freezer. When ice crystals begin to form 2 inches all around the edges of the pan, remove and stir until smooth. Return the pan to the freezer and repeat this process two more times, or until a smooth consistency has been reached.

Pack into plastic containers and store in the freezer. Remove about 10 minutes before serving to soften the ice slightly. Scoop into wineglasses or parfaits. Top with 1 tablespoon Calvados; garnish with an apple slice.

MAKES 5 CUPS, OR 12 TO 16 SMALL SERVINGS

Green Apple Cider Ice seems especially "right" at Christmas.

143

VICTORIAN SCRAP COOKIES

Victorian scrap cookies were popular in the 1800s. They were made by attaching scrap pictures to cookies with a bit of sugar and water. (The inedible pictures were removed before eating.) The method provided an extra dimension to cookie decoration and was also quick to do. Especially attractive cookies might be hung on the tree and saved from year to year.

This is a marvelous basic butter cookie recipe that I make year-round, cutting the dough in the shapes of the season and decorating accordingly—hearts in February with red sugar on top, shamrocks in March, turkeys in November. The dough must chill overnight and can be kept several days before rolling out.

2 cups all-purpose flour

1 teaspoon salt

1 cup (2 sticks) unsalted butter, at room temperature (no substitutes)

1 large egg

1 teaspoon vanilla extract

1 cup confectioners' sugar

assorted Victorian labels or decorating sugars

Royal Icing (page 96) or a stiff confectioners'-sugar-and-water mixture

Place the flour, salt, and butter in a food processor bowl; pulse until a soft crumbly dough is formed. Transfer to a large mixer bowl. In a small bowl, beat the egg and vanilla together until frothy; set aside.

Add the confectioners' sugar to the flour-butter mixture and combine. Add the egg mixture, but do not overmix. Cover and refrigerate overnight.

Remove the dough from the refrigerator 30 minutes before rolling out; on a lightly floured surface, roll out very thinly, about ⅛ inch thick, using as little flour as possible. Preheat the oven to 350° F.

Using decorative cutters (or ovals and squares cut from cardboard to fit the Victorian seals), cut out cookies and place them on parchment-lined cookie sheets. To reroll the leftover dough, you may have to refrigerate it or place it in the freezer for a few minutes. Avoid adding a lot of flour to the board, or the cookies will be tough.

Bake for 6 to 8 minutes, or until just barely colored, watching carefully, since the cookies can overbrown in a matter of seconds. Transfer immediately to paper-lined racks to cool. Attach the Victorian "scraps" or seals with icing or the sugar-water mixture. Store the cookies in tins, separated by layers of plastic wrap to prevent the butter from staining the "scraps." They can also be frozen.

Note: The recipe is easily doubled, but the dough must be processed in two batches.

MAKES 4 DOZEN COOKIES

Top to bottom: *Gingerbread Cakes, Victorian Scrap Cookies, and Chocolate Noëls.*

CHOCOLATE NOËLS

When I first tasted these cookies (some would call them confections) I assumed they must be time-consuming to make since they were so good. I couldn't have been more wrong. And I certainly did not guess that humble oatmeal was one of the ingredients. These are especially good with sorbets.

1 cup (2 sticks) unsalted butter
  (no substitutes)
2 7-ounce Hershey's milk chocolate bars with almonds
2½ cups quick-cooking oats
approximately 1½ cups confectioners' sugar

In the top of a double boiler, melt the butter and chocolate over simmering water. Blend with a whisk, then add the oats and combine well. Form big marble-size balls; this mixture is both crumbly and wet, and you don't think it is going to hold together, but it will. Be patient. Place in a wax-paper–lined pan and chill. When the cookies are firm, roll them in confectioners' sugar. Store them in the refrigerator, but allow them to come to room temperature 30 minutes before serving.

MAKES 4½ DOZEN COOKIES

GINGERBREAD CAKES

Not only is this a practical recipe, since the batter can be refrigerated, but it also is a velvety dark cake, aristocratic enough for the most sophisticated dessert tables. For the holidays, I bake the cake in two jelly-roll pans and, after baking, cut it with Christmas cookie cutters and sprinkle with confectioners' sugar. Other times of the year I bake the batter in a 9 x 13-inch pan and cut it in squares. Either could be served on individual dessert plates in a pool of crème anglaise. This is a very moist, fine-textured gingerbread. It should be served at room temperature for full flavor.

1 cup vegetable oil
1 cup (2 sticks) unsalted butter, at room temperature
1 cup firmly packed light brown sugar
1 cup light molasses
1 tablespoon ground ginger
1 tablespoon ground cinnamon
1 teaspoon salt
3 cups all-purpose flour
1 tablespoon baking soda
1 cup boiling water
2 large eggs, beaten

Preheat the oven to 325° F. In a large mixer bowl, beat the oil and butter, then add the brown sugar and continue beating until the mixture is fluffy. Blend in the molasses. Quickly mix in the spices and salt. Add the flour and blend. In a measuring cup, combine the baking soda and water, and add to the flour mixture. Blend until smooth, then mix in the eggs. At this point, the mixture can be used immediately or refrigerated for up to 5 days.

Divide the batter between two 10 x 15-inch jelly-roll pans and bake for 45 minutes, or until the top of the cake springs back when lightly touched with your finger and the sides of the cake have slightly pulled away from the sides of the pan. Cool and cut into desired shapes.

**MAKES ABOUT 3 DOZEN
3-INCH CAKES**

DRAMA QUARTETTE SUPPER WITH DESSERT BUFFET

Warm Beet Vichyssoise   Brie Wafers

Roast Duck with Rhubarb-Chutney Sauce

Green Beans with
Orange-Savory Vinaigrette

Wild Rice with Black Walnuts

Mushroom Tartlets

Tossed Winter Greens with Holiday Dressing

DESSERT BUFFET

Steamed Apple Pudding

Pecan Torte with Chocolate Glaze

Mousse-Filled Tulip Cups with
Raspberry Sauce

Christmas Pavlova

Cranberry Pecan Pie

WARM BEET VICHYSSOISE

Combining ruby-red beets with a well-seasoned potato soup base produces a sublimely deep pink and distinctively flavored soup that is delightful year-round. Serve this in clear glass bowls or punch cups to enjoy the color.

3 tablespoons unsalted butter

¾ cup chopped onion

3 medium potatoes, peeled and coarsely chopped

2 cups chicken stock

1 bay leaf

3 whole cloves

2 14-ounce cans beets, drained; or 4 large fresh beets, cooked, peeled, and chopped

1 tablespoon lemon juice

½ teaspoon bitters

½ teaspoon powdered vegetable seasoning

½ teaspoon salt

¼ teaspoon freshly ground white pepper

approximately 1½ cups half-and-half

fresh chives, for garnish

Melt the butter in a heavy saucepan and add the onion. Sauté until the onion is transparent; do not brown. Add the potatoes, stock, bay leaf, and cloves. Cover and bring to a boil, then lower the heat and simmer until the potatoes are tender, about 20 minutes. Cool slightly. Remove the bay leaf and cloves.

Meanwhile, in a food processor, puree the beets until completely smooth; transfer to another container. Without washing out the bowl, process the potato mixture until smooth, then add to the beets and combine thoroughly. Add the seasonings. At this point, the soup can be refrigerated overnight.

Before serving, heat the soup in a large saucepan and whisk in as much half-and-half as needed; do not boil. Garnish with chives.

MAKES 8 LARGE OR 14 TO 16
PUNCH-CUP SERVINGS

BRIE WAFERS

This is the perfect cocktail snack for Brie lovers—the soft wafers resemble delicate (unsweetened) cookies and are quite rich and very elegant.

½ pound Brie, at room temperature

1 cup (2 sticks) unsalted butter, at room temperature

2 cups all-purpose flour

¼ teaspoon cayenne pepper

¼ teaspoon salt

¼ teaspoon Worcestershire sauce

Combine the cheese and butter in a food processor and process until creamy. Add the flour, cayenne, salt, and Worcestershire sauce. Mix, pulsing on and off, until a very soft dough forms. Transfer the dough to a plate and shape into a log about 1½ inches in diameter. Wrap tightly in plastic and refrigerate overnight.

Preheat the oven to 375° F. Slice the dough into ¼-inch-thick rounds. Place on a parchment-lined baking sheet and bake for 7 to 8 minutes, or until lightly browned. Cool on a rack and store in an airtight tin.

MAKES 30 WAFERS

OPPOSITE: *Dramatic Mousse-Filled Tulip Cups.*

WILD RICE WITH BLACK WALNUTS

*The way rice has been dried and when it was
harvested will affect the cooking time, so watch it
and taste for tenderness. To increase the volume
and decrease the cooking time, soak the rice in
water for six hours or overnight; then drain off
the water and add fresh before cooking.*

1½ cups wild rice

4 cups water

1½ tablespoons balsamic vinegar

¼ cup (½ stick) unsalted butter, melted

½ cup chopped Italian parsley

1 cup toasted black walnuts

½ teaspoon vegetable seasoning, or to taste

½ teaspoon salt

¼ teaspoon freshly ground black pepper

Place the wild rice in a strainer and rinse thoroughly under cold running water. Bring the 4 cups of water to a full boil in a deep metal saucepan. Stir in the rice, reduce the heat, cover, and simmer for 35–40 minutes, or just until the kernels puff open. Uncover, fluff with a fork, and simmer 5 minutes longer. Drain off any excess liquid and transfer the rice to a heated bowl.

In the meantime, combine the remaining ingredients in a small bowl. Pour over the rice, toss with a fork to mix, and serve immediately.

MAKES 6 TO 8 SERVINGS

GREEN BEANS WITH ORANGE SAVORY VINAIGRETTE

*I like the appearance and texture of green beans
with the duck and wild rice. The notion of
reducing fruit juices before combining them with
the rest of the vinaigrette ingredients comes from
fellow cookbook writer and friend Stephen
Schmidt. I do hope you can find fresh savory for
this, but if not, you can get by with dried.*

¾ cup orange juice

1½ tablespoons lemon juice

grated zest of 1 orange

½ teaspoon salt

¼ teaspoon freshly ground black pepper

**3 teaspoons finely minced fresh savory, or
 ½ teaspoon dried**

½ cup walnut or safflower oil

**1½ pounds tender young green beans, snapped
 at the stem end**

In a small enamel or glass saucepan, combine the orange juice, lemon juice, and orange zest. Simmer uncovered over moderate heat until the juice is reduced to about 5 tablespoons, about 15 minutes; cool. Transfer to a glass jar and add the salt, pepper, savory, and oil. Top with a lid, shake vigorously, and set aside until ready to serve.

Bring at least 6 quarts of water to a rapid boil and drop in the beans. Boil rapidly, uncovered, for 4–7 minutes, or until the beans are tender but still firm to the bite. Immediately drain and transfer to a shallow bowl. Shake the vinaigrette again to recombine, and pour over the beans. Toss and serve at once.

MAKES 6 TO 8 SERVINGS

ROAST DUCK WITH RHUBARB-CHUTNEY SAUCE

If you are looking for an unusual entrée to serve at a holiday buffet, this recipe may just be it. Roast duckling, leaner than ever, is a smashing centerpiece, and this version with its chutney sauce is quite wonderful.

The ducks are rubbed first with cracked black pepper, then allowed to dry uncovered in the refrigerator, which makes the skin crispy when roasted. Accompanied by a rhubarb and red wine sauce with a touch of cumin, this duck dish has real panache. Serve it with a simple accompaniment of tender green beans.

DUCK

½ cup Chinese oyster sauce (available in Oriental markets and some supermarkets)

2 tablespoons honey

2 ducklings, 4½ pounds to 5 pounds each

½ cup cracked black peppercorns

3 tablespoons coarse salt

1¼ tablespoons dried rosemary

3 garlic cloves, peeled and finely minced

1½ tablespoons paprika

STOCK

2 carrots, cut into chunks

2 celery stalks, cut into chunks

1 large onion, quartered

2 bay leaves

10 whole cloves

10 black peppercorns

12 cups water

SAUCE

1 cup Spicy Rhubarb Chutney (page 109)

2 cups medium-dry red wine

½ teaspoon ground cumin

In a small bowl, combine the oyster sauce and honey. Rinse the ducks and pat dry, reserving the giblets for the stock. Cut off any excess inner fat and discard. Brush the ducks liberally with the honey mixture. Sprinkle the cracked pepper on a cutting board and roll the ducks in it until they are well coated. Place the ducks on racks and refrigerate, uncovered, for 2 days.

In a large stockpot, combine all of the stock ingredients, including the reserved giblets but not the liver. Cover, bring to a boil, lower heat, and simmer for 45 minutes. Strain through a sieve and refrigerate until ready to use.

Preheat the oven to 350° F. Combine the salt, rosemary, garlic, and paprika in a small bowl, rubbing the garlic into the dry seasonings. Season the ducks with the mixture, insert a meat thermometer into the fleshy part of one duck's thigh, and place on a wire rack in a large roasting pan. Bake for approximately 1½ hours, or until the temperature registers 160° F. and the legs move easily. Let the ducks rest 10 to 15 minutes before carving.

While the ducks roast, prepare the sauce. Combine the chutney and wine in a deep saucepan. Reduce the mixture by half, uncovered, over low heat, about 20 minutes. Add 2 cups of the reserved stock and continue cooking over low heat until the mixture thickens, about 1 hour longer. Add the cumin and simmer 5 minutes. The texture should be quite thick, not runny. Carve the duck, transfer to warmed plates, and spoon the sauce on the side.

MAKES 6 GENEROUS SERVINGS

MUSHROOM TARTLETS

Sometimes finding a new vegetable dish or meat accompaniment is a difficult task. Wanting something quite spiffy to go with the duck, I devised these little tartlets using dried and fresh mushrooms. The mixture can be made in advance, and so can the shells.

1 recipe Holiday Pastry (page 113)

1 cup chicken or beef stock

¼ cup dry sherry

1 ounce dried morel mushrooms (see Directory)

2 tablespoons olive oil

¼ cup minced onion

1 teaspoon minced garlic

1½ pounds thinly sliced white button mushrooms

¾ cup half-and-half

1 teaspoon rubbed sage

⅛ teaspoon Tabasco sauce

⅛ teaspoon bitters

⅛ teaspoon freshly ground black pepper

¼ teaspoon finely minced fresh parsley

Preheat the oven to 400° F. On a lightly floured cloth, roll out the pastry until ⅛ inch thick. Using a 4-inch cutter, cut out rounds and place in 24 tart pans. Bake 10 to 12 minutes, or until golden brown. Remove the shells from the pans and let cool. (Shells can be frozen. Reheat them on a cookie sheet in a 400° F. oven for about 5 minutes.)

In a medium saucepan, heat ¼ cup of the stock with the sherry until very hot but not boiling. Add the morels, cover, and allow to stand for 30 minutes, stirring occasionally. If the mushrooms are large, cut them into small pieces with scissors.

In a medium saucepan, heat the olive oil over medium heat, add the onion, and sauté for about 2 minutes, or until the onion begins to soften. Add the garlic and cook for 1 minute longer. Add the button mushrooms and morels with their soaking liquid. Simmer, uncovered,

for 10 to 12 minutes, or until all but 1 tablespoon of liquid has cooked away.

Add the half-and-half, remaining stock, sage, Tabasco, bitters, and pepper. Cook over medium heat for 12 to 15 minutes, or until the mixture is very thick. Stir in the parsley. (This mixture can be made up to 2 days in advance, covered, and refrigerated. Reheat in a saucepan over medium-low heat.)

Spoon 1 heaping teaspoon of filling into each warmed shell and serve.

MAKES 24 TARTLETS

HOLIDAY DRESSING FOR WINTER GREENS

This is a most attractive dressing with a pronounced tarragon flavor. Serve it over mixed greens with either red onion rings or ruby-tipped lettuce. It is also a lively accompaniment to cold sliced chicken.

⅓ cup white wine or tarragon vinegar

1¼ teaspoons dry mustard

1¼ teaspoons dried savory

1¼ teaspoons dried tarragon, or 1 tablespoon finely minced fresh

1¼ teaspoons dried thyme

½ cup chopped onion

⅓ cup chopped fresh parsley

½ teaspoon salt

¼ teaspoon freshly ground white pepper

¼ teaspoon Tabasco sauce

1¼ cups lightly flavored vegetable oil

In a food processor or blender, combine all the ingredients except the oil. With the machine running, add the oil in a slow stream until the mixture emulsifies. Transfer to a glass jar, cover tightly, and refrigerate until serving time.

MAKES A SCANT 2 CUPS

Mushroom Tartlets combine flavorful dried Michigan morels with less costly cultivated mushrooms.

A bowl of Calvados-flavored hard sauce accompanies the satisfying Steamed Apple Pudding.

STEAMED APPLE PUDDING

This is a very elegant dish, similar to a Victorian steamed pudding, and though it contains no suet, it has the same fabled richness of a suet pudding. Serve this dramatic and satisfying affair surrounded by lemon leaves and on a Victorian cake dish.

4 tablespoons (½ stick) unsalted butter, at room temperature

½ cup firmly packed light brown sugar

½ cup molasses

1 large egg

1 tablespoon grated lemon zest

1 teaspon vanilla extract

2 cups all-purpose flour

2 teaspoons baking powder

½ teaspoon ground allspice

½ teaspoon ground cinnamon

½ teaspoon ground ginger

½ teaspoon mace

¾ teaspoon salt

½ cup buttermilk

1 cup peeled and finely chopped apples, such as McIntosh or Northern Spy

½ cup coarsely chopped black walnuts

Calvados Hard Sauce (page 115) or crème anglaise

In a large mixer bowl, cream the butter and brown sugar for 1 minute. Add the molasses, egg, lemon zest, and vanilla; blend well.

In a large bowl, stir together the dry ingredients. Add them to the butter mixture on low speed, alternating with the buttermilk and beginning and ending with the dry ingredients. Beat in the apples and nuts, and pour into a greased and floured 7-cup steamed pudding mold. Cover tightly.

Place pudding on a rack in a deep kettle and add enough water to reach halfway up the sides of the mold. Bring the water to a boil, cover the pot, and steam the pudding for 1½ hours, replenishing the water as needed and keeping it at a brisk but not rolling boil.

Remove the mold from the kettle, uncover, and allow the pudding to rest for 10 minutes. Loosen the edges with a knife and tip the pudding out onto a round platter. Cut into wedges and serve hot with hard sauce or crème anglaise.

Note: The pudding may be made up to a month in advance and kept tightly wrapped in foil, frozen. Reheat the frozen pudding, wrapped in foil, in a preheated 325° F. oven for 1 hour.

MAKES 8 TO 10 SERVINGS

MOUSSE-FILLED TULIP CUPS WITH RASPBERRY SAUCE

Silky and luxurious, this mousse is also delicious served in crystal glasses with dark chocolate sauce.

8 ounces white chocolate (see Note)
½ cup (1 stick) unsalted butter
6 large egg yolks
½ cup white crème de cacao
1 quart heavy cream
2 tablespoons light corn syrup
¼ cup confectioners' sugar
14 Chocolate Tulips (page 154)
Red Raspberry Sauce (recipe follows)
Chocolate Stamens (page 159)

Place the white chocolate and butter in the top of a double boiler and melt over simmering water. Remove the top pan from the boiler and set it aside to cool slightly, about 5 minutes.

In a mixer bowl, beat the egg yolks for 1 minute; stir in the crème de cacao. Stir the egg yolks into the white chocolate; refrigerate until cool, about 45 minutes.

In a chilled mixer bowl, combine the cream, corn syrup, and confectioners' sugar. Beat until stiff. Fold in the cooled chocolate mixture. Transfer to a large compote and chill until serving time. To serve, fill each tulip cup with a dollop of mousse, place on a dessert plate, and spoon some raspberry sauce around the cup. Tuck a chocolate stamen into the top of each mousse.

Note: I use 7 Nestlé's Alpine white chocolate bars when bulk white chocolate is unavailable.

MAKES 12 TO 16 SERVINGS

Red Raspberry Sauce

This sprightly bright red sauce is quick to make and can also be used on rice puddings, cheesecake, sorbets, and ice cream.

1 10-ounce package frozen raspberries, thawed
1 12-ounce jar seedless raspberry preserves
¼ cup kirsch or light rum

Press the raspberries through a fine sieve, extracting all the juice; discard the seeds. To the juice, add the preserves and rum; refrigerate until needed.

MAKES 1¾ CUPS

CHOCOLATE TULIPS

These gloriously dramatic chocolate cups made of pink, white, and dark chocolate resemble mottled Rembrandt tulips. Fill the tulips with White Chocolate Mousse (page 153), garnish with a chocolate stamen (page 159), add some Red Raspberry Sauce (page 153), and you have a knock-out dessert.

They take a bit of practice, but after doing a few, the process moves along rather quickly. The tulips can be made a week in advance and stored in a cool place.

Here are some hints to make this a smooth operation:

1. For best results, buy the chocolate from a candy-making supply store (or see the Directory). Check your Yellow Pages and ask for compound chocolate or coating chocolate in assorted colors. This recipe can be halved, but to ensure enough perfect cups, I advise the 1-pound increments.

2. Use smaller balloons. Since I serve the tulips as part of a dessert buffet, I don't want the cups overly large. This does work with any size balloon, but the most manageable is the 4-inch size, also called a water balloon. I have used various sizes, up to 7 inches. Be sure they are fully blown up and tightly knotted.

3. To make sure that the chocolate will stick to the balloons, be careful that no water gets into the chocolate; this might happen if the double boiler lid is on and condensation drips down into the melting chocolate. Also resist the temptation to coat the balloons with vegetable spray. The chocolate will not adhere to a greased balloon.

MATERIALS/INGREDIENTS
1 pound white compound coating
1 pound deep rose compound coating
1 pound dark chocolate compound coating

TOOLS/EQUIPMENT
3 double boilers
3 wooden spoons
3 rubber spatulas
24 4-inch balloons (water balloons)
4 or 5 large cookie sheets
wax paper or parchment paper
½ cup measuring cup

1. In the double boilers, melt each of the chocolates separately over simmering water. Fully blow up the balloons, knot or tie firmly, and set aside. Cover the cookie sheets with wax or parchment paper. Cover additional cookie sheets with wax paper for storing the balloons.

2. When the chocolate is melted, use a ½-cup measure to pour out a 3-inch-wide strip of white chocolate—it should be about 10 inches long—on a covered cookie sheet.

3. Right beside it, pour out a 3 x 10-inch strip of dark chocolate, and next to that, a strip of the rose, and a final one of the white. Work quickly, since the chocolate will begin to cool immediately. (Not to worry if you are using more white chocolate than the dark and rose; you'll have chocolate left over anyway.) If there are two of you working, set up 2 pans for rolling the balloons.

4. Hold a balloon by the stem and, dipping only the lower third of the balloon into the chocolates, tip it back and forth in all 3 colors to form about 5 or 6 petals. Don't cover the balloon too high—not beyond the curve—or the chocolate will crack when you are loosening the petals. Continue in that way all the way around the balloon, rocking the balloon in the chocolate to make sure the bottom is heavily covered. Keep the extra chocolate warm over low heat and replenish the strips as needed, also using a clean pan if needed.

5. Place the coated balloons on the prepared

cookie sheets, repeating until you have as many tulip cups as desired. Make a few extra, since some will not come off the balloons in perfect shape, and set in a cool place (this can be the garage or the refrigerator). Allow them to stand until firm, about 1 hour out of the refrigerator or 15 minutes in the refrigerator. Return the balloons to room temperature before deflating.

6. Very carefully, using your fingers, press the balloon away slightly from the chocolate all the way around the top of the flower. Untie

the balloon carefully, holding the air in with your fingers, then *slowly* release the air in little spurts. Keep the top twisted to control the flow of air, all the time easing the balloon away from the petals. It may cling quite firmly to the bottom, so tug it gently for the final release; you may even have to use the tip of a knife to remove it.

7. Store the tulip cups on the prepared sheets in a cool dry place.

MAKES ABOUT 2 DOZEN CUPS

CRANBERRY PECAN PIE

This is a most attractive pie, with a whorl of pecan halves decorating the top. The texture is similar to a pecan pie, yet the lilting flavor of the cranberries makes it nicely Christmasy.

Holiday Pastry (page 113) for a 1-crust pie

1 cup fresh or frozen cranberries

3 large eggs

⅔ cup sugar

1 cup dark corn syrup

6 tablespoons (¾ stick) unsalted butter, melted

1 teaspoon vanilla extract

¼ teaspoon mace

speck of salt

¾ to 1 cup pecan halves

Roll out the pie crust until ⅛ inch thick and press into a 9-inch pie pan. Flute the edges and set aside.

Preheat the oven to 350° F. (325° if using a glass pan). Process the cranberries until finely chopped; arrange over the bottom of the pie shell and set aside. In a large mixer bowl, beat the eggs until frothy. Mix in the sugar, corn syrup, butter, vanilla, mace, and salt.

Pour the egg mixture over the cranberries. Arrange the pecan halves on top of the pie in circles, beginning with the outer edge and working toward the center, covering it completely. Bake for 45 to 50 minutes, or until the pie is golden brown and almost set—it will still be a little shaky but will firm up as it cools.

Note: If you are making a 10-inch pie, prepare 1½ batches of filling and bake at 325° F. for 45 minutes, then cover lightly with foil and continue baking 30 minutes longer, or until golden brown.

MAKES 8 SERVINGS

CHRISTMAS PAVLOVA

Pavlova was a popular Russian ballerina, especially famous for her "Dying Swan" in the ballet Swan Lake. *This dessert was named in her honor after she appeared in Australia and New Zealand. The tartness of the bright red sauce is a perfect counterpoint to the sweet white smoothness of the meringue. It is a smashingly dramatic dessert, and very simple to prepare.*

8 jumbo egg whites, at room temperature

¼ teaspoon cream of tartar

¼ teaspoon salt

2 cups superfine sugar

1 teaspoon vanilla extract

1 teaspoon almond extract

4 teaspoons cornstarch

2 cups heavy cream

sugar to taste (optional)

3 cups pureed and strained raspberries or strawberries, sweetened to taste

fresh mint sprigs, for garnish

Preheat the oven to 385° F. (400° F. is just a bit too hot and would tint the meringue). In a large mixer bowl, combine the egg whites, cream of tartar, and salt and beat on medium speed until the egg whites become stiff. Add the sugar, a little at a time, beating constantly, then beat in the extracts. The egg whites should be glossy and peak stiffly. Gradually beat in the cornstarch.

Coat a 10-inch pie pan with vegetable spray, and spread the meringue in it, mounding it up in the middle. Place the pavlova in the oven, immediately turn off the heat, and let it stand in the oven for 1 hour. Then open the door completely and let the pavlova remain in the oven until it is completely cool.

To serve, whip the cream and sweeten it if you like. Pipe or spread the whipped cream over the pavlova. Place a bit more than 2 tablespoons of fruit puree on the bottom of a dessert plate and top with a wedge of pavlova. Garnish with fresh mint.

MAKES 12 SERVINGS

PECAN TORTE WITH CHOCOLATE GLAZE

I served this dessert at the very first dinner party I gave after I was married. To me, it is as pleasing now as it was then. The torte can be made way ahead and frozen, and the filling and frosting are a snap to do the day of the party. The torte does fall slightly in the middle; you can compensate for it by mounding the whipped cream filling up a bit in the slight depression of the bottom layer.

TORTE

4 large eggs, at room temperature, separated
1 cup granulated sugar
2 tablespoons sifted cake flour
½ teaspoon salt
½ teaspoon baking powder
1 tablespoon orange juice or white rum
2 cups very finely ground pecans

FILLING

½ cup heavy cream
1½ teaspoons grated orange zest
½ teaspoon vanilla extract
¼ cup confectioners' sugar
1 teaspoon light corn syrup

FROSTING

6 ounces semisweet chocolate morsels
½ cup sour cream
speck of salt
Chocolate Leaves (recipe follows) or chopped pistachio nuts, for garnish

Preheat the oven to 350° F. In a mixer bowl, beat the egg yolks until thick and light, about 2 minutes. Gradually add the granulated sugar, and then beat for another 2 minutes so the mixture is well combined. By hand, stir in the cake flour, salt, baking powder, and juice or rum.

In another mixer bowl, beat the egg whites until very stiff. Fold half of the nuts into the yolk mixture, then add half of the egg whites to the egg-nut mixture and repeat, ending with the egg whites. Pour into 2 well-greased 8-inch cake pans and bake for 25 to 30 minutes, or until the tops are golden brown and spring back when lightly touched with your finger. Cool on a rack for 20 minutes, then remove from the pans.

To make the filling, pour the cream into a chilled mixer bowl and add the orange zest, vanilla, confectioners' sugar, and corn syrup. Beat until stiff. Place one cake layer on a round plate and spread with all the filling. Top with the remaining layer and refrigerate.

Melt the chocolate morsels in a double boiler over hot, not boiling, water. Stir in the sour cream and salt, and mix gently. Remove from the heat and spread on the sides and top of the torte. Garnish with chocolate leaves, or sprinkle with chopped pistachios.

MAKES 10 SERVINGS

Chocolate Leaves or Stamens

¼ cup semisweet chocolate morsels
½ teaspoon unsalted butter or margarine
12 rose leaves or other small leaves

To make leaves, melt the chocolate morsels and butter or margarine in a double boiler over hot, not boiling, water. Use a small, clean paintbrush to paint the chocolate very thickly over the backs of the leaves, about ⅛ inch thick, bringing the chocolate just to the edges. Chill in the refrigerator until very firm. Peel off the chocolate leaves and store in the freezer.

To make stamens, place just the chocolate morsels in a small plastic bag. Close it tightly and place in a small bowl of hot water. When the chocolate is melted, about 5 minutes, remove from the water, blot the bag dry, and with a pair of scissors, cut off a tiny snip of one corner (about ⅛ inch). Squeeze out small squiggles or loops on a piece of parchment paper. Refrigerate until firm.

MAKES 12 LEAVES OR 6 TO 9 STAMENS

CHRISTMAS TREE

As it is brought in with its coat
Smelling of wilderness and yet not furry,
It still has an untamed look,
As if it might crash the ceiling
Or lie down in a corner and refuse
All welcome, an unwilling prisoner.
Small children and animals are wary
For fear it might break out or simply die,
Until it is time to set it up on end,
Sturdy, sweet-smelling, and so high
It makes a shelter and becomes a friend.

This is the moment to uncover
In boxes so light, what can they hold?
From softest tissue to unwrap and gather
The apples of silver, the apples of gold.
Now gently deck the boughs, gently unfurl
The sprung branch that will wear

This lightest jewel in its pungent fur.
Is it real? Will it stay? Has it come
From so far, long ago, just to bloom
Just tonight, heart's desire, in this room?
The candles are lit, one by one very slowly.
All gaze; all are silent; each child is holy.
The smallest in pajamas goes and lies
Under the boughs with dazzled open eyes,
And as he looks up at the gaudy toys
They become strange and spiritual joys,
While the tree, stranger once from wilderness,
Is an angelic presence that can bless;
And, all wound round now with the blazing
   truth,
The boy, the tree together are redeeming myth.

May Sarton
As Does New Hampshire, 1967

Food Sources by Mail

Antique apples, over 50 varieties, including Black Gillyflower and White Winter Permain. Holiday gift packages and mail order shipping.
Doud Nurseries
Route #1, Denver, IN 46926
317-985-3937

Dried cherries, blueberries, cranberries, morel mushrooms, fine assortment of unusual jams, jellies, and condiments—the best of Michigan. Nice gift boxes made of local white birch bark available. Write for handsome catalog.
American Spoon Foods
1668 Clarion Avenue
Petoskey, MI 49770-0566
616-347-9030

Chocolate coating compound and royal icing mix, plus special food flavors—pecan, butter, black walnut, etc. Phone or write for information.
Country Kitchen Retail Mail Order
3225 Wells Street
Fort Wayne, IN 46808
219-482-4835

Honey-Baked Ham, smoked turkey, and other specialty meats and very nice gift packages. This ham is spiral cut, fully cooked, and glazed with honey and brown sugar—it is ideal for entertaining and gift giving. Write or phone for illustrated brochure.
HoneyBaked Foods, Inc.
P.O. Box 7043
Troy, MI 48077-7043
800-892-4267

Moravian mints. A holiday specialty—delicate minty sugar patties in four pastel colors and flavors. This shop also stocks unusual Christmas tree ornaments and small clip-on candles as pictured on page 41. Write or phone for information.
The Moravian Book Store
428 Main Street
Bethlehem, PA 18018
215-865-3823

Persimmon pulp, sweetened and canned for puddings, available by mail. Write for price list.
Dymple's Delight
Route #4, Box 53
Mitchell, IN 47446

Dried pomegranates and other herbal supplies.
Greenfield Herb Garden
Box 437
Shipshawana, IN 46565
219-768-7110

Wild rice. Call or write for free catalog, listing rice assortments, teas, recipe books, and other regional specialties.
The Wisconsin Gift Gallery
2579 University Avenue
Madison, WI
800-369-7423

Crafts and Folk Art

Arks, custom-made wooden. One of the top ark makers in the country; their arks are considered investment pieces.
Vaillancourt Folk Art
Sutton, MA

Candles (hand dipped) and molded beeswax ornaments, delicately golden and slow burning.
Mr. and Mrs. Robert Smith
1915 Kenmore Avenue
Bethlehem, PA 18018

Cast-iron candy molds, antique and reproductions, plus instructions and recipes. Molds range in price from $50 to $75. Send self-addressed stamped envelope for further information.
Mrs. Albert Dudrear, Jr.
144 East Springettsbury Avenue
York, PA 17403
717-843-6774
717-845-6420

Folk art and American antiques, Victorian dishes, and accoutrements.

BC Antiques
3461 Sandpoint Road
Fort Wayne, IN 46807
219-747-0043

Folk art, including Amish antiques, quilts, antique toys, doll houses, bird houses, and many country primitives.

Green Meadow Bed and Breakfast and Antique Shop
Route #2, Box 592
Shipshewana, IN 46565
219-768-4221

Folk art, including hand-carved and painted Santas, American and Russian versions, plus angels, painted wooden decorative Christmas boxes, etc. Write for catalog.

Winterwind Folk Arts Ltd.
Highway 261 West, Box 271
Lester Prairie, MN 55354

Herbal Christmas wreaths, swags, handmade ornaments, original carved Santas, and other folk art pieces, as featured on pages 1–31. Write or phone for information.

The Summer House
Route #4, Box 134
North Manchester, IN 46962
219-982-4707

MISCELLANEOUS

Cookware of all description. A marvelous shop— there isn't a thing this place doesn't have. Steamed pudding molds, Moravian half-moon cake pans (12-inch ribbed loaf pans), pastry forks, oversize cake pans. Located in the Italian Market section of Philadelphia. If you are there, don't miss it. Will ship anywhere.

Fantes
1006 South Ninth Street
Philadelphia, PA 19147
800-878-5557

Christmas china, red-speckled with Amish design (page 138).

M. Dallas Company
Howard, OH 43028

Wrapping papers and tags reproduced from authentic Victorian and early American designs. Write or call for information.

Melissa Neufield
P.O. Box 794
Diabolo, CA 94528
415-831-3494

Paperwhite narcissus and lilies-of-the-valley. Excellent mail order services and fine-quality bulbs. Good gift ideas. Write for information.

White Flower Farms
Litchfield, CT 06759

Pickle Christmas tree ornaments and other unusual gift items. One set of two: $12.50.

Winterthur Mail Order
100 Enterprise Place
Dover, Delaware 19901
800-767-0500

Write or phone for tourist information and list of holiday events.

Bethlehem Chamber of Commerce
459 Old York Road
Bethlehem, PA 18018
215-867-3788

The Bethlehem Inn Bed and Breakfast
476 New Street
Bethlehem, PA 18018
215-867-4985

····· **C R E D I T S** ·····

To all the wonderful people and organizations who shared their recipes, time, belongings, and ideas to make this book and the TV special happen, thank you: Ace Hardware, *Winona Lake, Indiana* • Kim and Rachel Agretto • Allen County Public Library, *Fort Wayne, Indiana* • Peggy Anderson • Norma Beadie • Bethlehem Chamber of Commerce • The Bethlehem Inn Bed and Breakfast • Betty's Antiques, *Fort Wayne, Indiana* • Noreen Brown • Jim Brubaker of Saxton's Nurseries, *New Haven, Indiana* • Gail Bryan • Dr. Douglas Caldwell, Central Moravian Church • Bruce Chaney of BC Antiques, *Fort Wayne, Indiana* • Sue Clutter • Crestwood Village Framing Shop, *Roanoke, Indiana* • M. Dallas Company, *Howard, Ohio* • Cidney Dillman • Doud Nursery and Antique Apples • Albert Dudrear, Jr. • Reba Dunmire • Samantha Eaton • Joan Fackler • *Fort Wayne Journal Gazette* • Pearl Frantz • *The Globe-Times, Bethlehem, Pennsylvania* • Greenfield Herb Garden, *Shipshewana, Indiana* • Green Meadow Bed and Breakfast and Gift Shop, *Shipshewana, Indiana* • Susi Griffiths • Suzanne Hall • Lois Hamilton • Oris and Kerry Hippensteel • Judy Hughes • Ike's Daughter's Antiques, *Silver Lake, Indiana* • Ellen and George Japps • Lois, Jessica, and Ryan Kendrick • Alice and Francis Knouss • Tina, Chloe, and Gary Lallo • Longaberger Basket Co., *Dresden, Ohio* • Lost and Found Antique Shop, *Bethlehem, Pennsylvania* • Dr. Roger, Susan, Emily, and Katie Martin • George, Linda, and Angie Mattes • Laura McCaffrey • David Merritt, Director of Music, *Central Moravian Church* • Patty Metzger • Mrs. Richard Michael • Ruth Miller • Moravian Academy • Moravian Central Church • Tony Murphy of Finer Things, *Oakland, California* • Josh Myers • Joyce Ochs • Gretchen and Mark Parseghian • James W. Peterson of Ocean Spray Cranberries, Inc. • John Pulver • Kristy Schmitt • Eva Slayton • Lucille and Bob Smith • Sara Spires • Betty S. Stewart • Vangie Sweitzer • Mary Kathryn Van Horn • Mike, Donna, and Michael Viglianti • Robert, Suzanne, and Calvin Virgilio • Scott, Jan, Andrew, and William Walker • Winterwind Folk Arts Ltd. • Mary Ellen, Eric, Kyle, and Sarah Zeiger •

Anglican Mincemeat Tarts, 112
APEAS Cookies, 56
Appetizers
  Brie Wafers, 147
  Cheese Lace Wafers, 139
Apple
  Cider Ice, Green, 142
  Maple Compote with Caraway
    Seeds, 31
  Pudding, Steamed, 152
Applesauce and Cinnamon
  Ornaments, 92

Bacon, Canadian, Orange-Glazed, with
  Cardamom, 28
Beef Tenderloin, Italian Stuffed, with
  Roasted Red Pepper and Garlic
  Sauce, 72
Beeswax crafts (candles), 65
Beet Vichyssoise, Warm, 147
Beverages
  Pineapple Spiced Cider, 24
  Raspberry Shrub, 23
  Rumrousal, 78
  Syllabub, 106
  Thomas Jefferson's Hot
    Chocolate, 57
Bibb Lettuce, Orange, and Red Onion
  Salad with Orange Dressing, 142
Bird Christmas Treats, 123
Bird Wreaths, Gourmet, 122
Biscotti, 78
Biscuits, Hot, 109
Bowl of cheer, 79
Bread. See Biscuits; Cornsticks;
  Muffins; Popovers; Welsh Cakes
Brie Wafers, 147
Brunch, Farmhouse, 22–31
Buns, Love, 55
Butter Semmels, 55

Cake(s)
  Gingerbread, 145
  Half-Moon or Winter, 53
  Moravian Suger, 54; Butter
    Semmels, 55; Love Buns, 55
  Pecan Torte with Chocolate
    Glaze, 158
Calvados Hard Sauce, 115
Canadian Bacon, Orange-Glazed, with
  Cardamom, 28
Canadian Pork Pie (Tourtière), 140
Candied Orange Peel, 116
Candles, beeswax crafts, 65
Candy(ies)
  Candied Orange Peel, 116
  Clear Toy (Lollipops,
    Sugarplums), 98
  hard, 99

Cheese Lace Wafers, 139
Cherry. See Dried Cherry
Chocolate
  Hot, Thomas Jefferson's, 57
  Leaves or Stamens, 159
  Noëls, 145
  Tulips, 154
Christmas. See Cookies; Decorations;
  Tree, etc.
Chutney. See also Relish
  Spicy Rhubarb, 109
Cider, Green Apple, Ice, 142
Compote, Maple Apple with Caraway
  Seeds, 31
Cookie(s)
  APEAS, 56
  Biscotti, 78
  Chocolate Noëls, 145
  Christmas, hints for, 50
  Christmas Tea After Moravian
    Vespers, 48–57
  Gingerbread Ark and Animals, 95
  Gingerbread Bowl, Christmas, 62
  Gingersnap Stained-Glass, 66
  Moravian Ginger Thins, 49
  Moravian Sand Tarts, 50
  Scottish Shortbread, 31
  Strawberry Heart, 116
  Victorian Scrap, 144
Cornmeal, Polenta Stars, 71
Cornsticks, Savory, 28
Cranberry Pecan Pie, 156

Decoration(s)
  apple ornaments, 21
  Applesauce and Cinnamon
    Ornaments, 92
  beeswax crafts (candles), 65
  Bird Christmas Treats, 123
  Bird Wreaths, Gourmet, 122
  Christmas Snow for Window
    Decorating, 64
  Christmas Stars, 127
  Christmas tree ornaments, 126
  feather trees, 9–10
  forcing branches, 120
  Gingerbread Ark and Animals, 95
  greens, Christmas, 89
  Herbal Wreath, Fresh, 14
  Holiday Topiaries, 129
  Indiana Hydrangea Balls, 128
  Moravian Mint Cones, 45
  Polly Heckewelder dolls, 39
  putzes (Nativity scenes), 36
  Royal Icing, 96
  Santa Claus, 2
  Toy Candy, Clear, 98

Victorian Hand Tree Ornaments, 13
Victorian pickle Christmas
  ornament, 101
Desserts. See also Cakes; Cookies
  Apple Pudding, Steamed, 152
  Chocolate Tulips, 154
  Christmas Pavlova, 157
  Cranberry Pecan Pie, 156
  Maple Apple Compote with Caraway
    Seeds, 31
  Mincemeat Tarts, Anglican, 112
  Mousse-Filled Tulip Cups with
    Raspberry Sauce, 153
  Pecan Torte with Chocolate
    Glaze, 158
  Persimmon Christmas Pudding,
    Steamed, with Nutmeg Hard
    Sauce, 114
  Victorian Sherry Jelly with Orange
    and Brandy, 110
  Zuccotto, 77
Dinner in Front of the Fireplace,
  138–45
Dressing, Holiday, for Winter
  Greens, 150
Dried Cherry and Wild Rice
  Muffins, 27
Drinks. See Beverages
Duck Roast, with Rhubarb-Chutney
  Sauce, 149

Eggs, Baked Country, with
  Mushrooms, 24

Farmhouse Brunch, 22–31
Feather trees, 9–10
Forcing branches (for decorations), 120

Gift Wrapping, Christmas, 124
Ginger Thins, Moravian, 49
Gingerbread, 95
  Ark and Animals, 95
  Bowl, Christmas (for cookies), 62
  Cakes, 145
Gingersnap Stained-Glass Cookies, 66
Green Apple Cider Ice, 142
Green Beans with Orange Savory
  Vinaigrette, 148
Greens
  Christmas, 89
  Winter, Holiday Dressing for, 150

Half-Moon Cakes or Winter
  Cakes, 53
Hand Tree Ornaments, Victorian, 13
Hard candies, about, 99
Hard Sauce, Nutmeg, 115;
  Calvados, 115
Herb Popovers, Simply Marvelous, 27

Herbal Wreath, Fresh, 14
Herbs at Christmas, 14
Holiday
    Dressing for Winter Greens, 150
    Pastry, 113
    Topiaries, 129
Honey, Spiced, 17
Hot Chocolate, Thomas Jefferson's, 57
Hydrangea Balls, Indiana, 128

Ice, Green Apple Cider, 142
Icing, Royal (for decorations), 96
Indiana Hydrangea Balls, 128
Italian
    Beef Tenderloin, Stuffed, with
        Roasted Red Pepper and Garlic
        Sauce, 72
    Biscotti, 78
    Polenta Stars, 71
    Zuccotto, 77

Jelly, Victorian Sherry, with Orange
    and Brandy, 110

Lollipops, Clear Toy Candy, 98
Love Buns, 55
Lovefeasts, 37

Maple Apple Compote with Caraway
    Seeds, 31
Mincemeat Tarts, Anglican, 112
Moravian
    beeswax crafts, 65
    Ginger Thins, 49
    lovefeasts, 37
    Mint Cones, 45
    Polly Heckewelder dolls, 39
    Sand Tarts, 50
    Sugar Cake, 54; Butter Semmels,
        55; Love Buns, 55
    traditions, 33–46
    Tree-Trimming Party Menu, 70–78
    Vespers, Christmas Cookie Tea
        After, 48–57
Mousse-Filled Tulip Cups with
    Raspberry Sauce, 153
Muffins, Wild Rice and Dried
    Cherry, 27
Multifloral Vinegar, 16
Mushroom Tartlets, 150

Nativity scenes (putzes), 36
Nutmeg Hard Sauce, 115
Nuts, Victorian Spiced, 105

Orange
    Dressing, Red Onion, and Bibb
        Lettuce Salad with, 142
    -Glazed Canadian Bacon with
        Cardamom, 28
    Peel, Candied, 116

Ornaments, See Decorations
Oyster Bisque, Creamy, 107

Pastry, Holiday, 113
Pavlova, Christmas, 157
Pecan
    Cranberry Pie, 156
    Torte with Chocolate Glaze, 158
Persimmon Christmas Pudding,
    Steamed, with Nutmeg Hard
    Sauce, 114
Pie
    Canadian Pork (Tourtière), 140
    Cranberry Pecan, 156
Pineapple Spiced Cider, 24
Polenta Stars, 71
Polly Heckewelder dolls, 39
Popovers, Simply Marvelous Herb, 27
Pork Pie, Canadian (Tourtière), 140
Pudding
    Christmas, about, 115
    Steamed Apple, 152
    Steamed Persimmon Christmas with
        Nutmeg Hard Sauce, 114
Punch bowl (bowl of cheer), 79
Putzes (Nativity scenes), 36

Raspberry
    Sauce, Red, 153
    Shrub, 23
Readings, Christmas, 137
Relish. See also Chutney
    Green Apple Cider Ice, 142
Rhubarb Chutney, Spicy, 109
Rice. See Wild Rice
Royal Icing (for decoration), 96
Rumrousal, 78

Salad
    Orange, Red Onion, and
        Bibb Lettuce, with Orange
        Dressing, 142
    Winter Greens, Tossed Fresh, with
        Cumin Vinaigrette, 73
Sauce
    Nutmeg Hard, 115; Calvados, 115
    Red Raspberry, 153
Scottish Shortbread, 31
Semmels, Butter, 55
Shortbread, Scottish, 31
Shrub, Raspberry, 23
Snow, Christmas, for Window
    Decorating, 64
Soup
    Beet Vichyssoise, Warm, 147
    Oyster Bisque, Creamy, 107
Spiced
    Cider, Pineapple, 24
    Honey, 17
    Nuts, Victorian, 105

Spicy Rhubarb Chutney, 109
Stars, Christmas, 127
Steamed Pudding. See Pudding
Strawberry Heart Cookies, 116
Sugar Cake, Moravian, 54; Butter
    Semmels, 55; Love Buns, 55
Sugarplums, Clear Toy Candy, 98
Supper
    Christmas Eve, 104–17
    Drama Quartette, with Dessert
        Buffet, 146–59
Syllabub, 106

Tartlets, Mushroom, 150
Tarts
    Anglican Mincemeat, 112
    Moravian Sand, 50
Tea, Christmas Cookie, after Moravian
    Vespers, 48–57
Thomas Jefferson's Hot Chocolate, 57
Topiaries, Holiday, 129
Torte, Pecan, with Chocolate
    Glaze, 158
Tourtière (Canadian Pork Pie), 140
Toy Candy, Clear, 98
Traditions. See Moravian; Victorian
Tree, Christmas
    ornaments, 126
    -Trimming Party, 70–79
    A Victorian legacy, 102
Tulips, Chocolate, 154
Tysen Cymreeg (Welsh Cakes), 74

Vichyssoise, Warm Beet, 147
Victorian
    Christmas Eve Supper, 104–17
    Christmas greens, stories of, 89
    Hand Tree Ornaments, 13
    legacy (Christmas tree), 102
    pickle Christmas ornament, 101
    Scrap Cookies, 144
    Sherry Jelly with Orange and
        Brandy, 110
    Spiced Nuts, 105
    traditions, 81–88
Vinegar, Multifloral, 16

Welsh Cakes (Tysen Cymreeg), 74
Wild Rice
    with Black Walnuts, 148
    and Dried Cherry Muffins, 27
Winter Cakes or Half-Moon Cakes, 53
Winter Greens, Tossed Fresh, with
    Cumin Vinaigrette, 73
Wrapping, Christmas gift, 124
Wreath, Fresh Herbal, 14
Wreaths, Gourmet Bird, 122

Zuccotto, 77